Encounters

with

Dylan

Encounters with Dylan

Edited by Jon Gower

with a Foreword by Ali Anwar

The Poetry Foundation
Y Sefydliad Barddoniaeth

Cover photograph of Dylan Thomas,
Millbrook, New York, 1952
by Rollie McKenna
© Rosalie Thorne McKenna Foundation 2014
Courtesy Center for Creative Photography
University of Arizona Foundation

ISBN: 978-0-9927560-2-4

Acknowledgements are due to Orion Publishing for permission to reproduce quotations from the poems 'Author's Prologue', 'Being But Men', 'A Refusal to Mourn the Death, By Fire, of a Child in London', 'Especially When the October Wind' and 'I See the Boys of Summer'. The extracts from *Under Milk Wood* are used courtesy of J.M. Dent along with an extract from 'Quite Early One Morning' which first appeared in *Quite Early One Morning: Broadcasts by Dylan Thomas*.

Typeset and designed by Dafydd Prys
Printed in Wales by Gwasg Gomer, Llandysul

Published by The H'mm Foundation, Grove Extension – Room 426, Swansea University, Singleton Park, Swansea SA2 8PP

Contents

Foreword

Ali Anwar, CEO H'mm Foundation

I'm delighted to provide the foreword to this collection of essays about one of my favourite poets, Dylan Thomas, which is published by the H'mm Foundation during the centennial celebrations of his birth. I found his poetry most interesting although I haven't had the opportunity to study it too deeply or, indeed write about his work myself. I am however in the process of commissioning this collection of 'encounters' to be translated to Arabic, and I'm hopeful of its success.

The first time I encountered the name Dylan Thomas was seeing it on an accommodation advert placed on the window of the Uplands Bookshop in Swansea. It was in the late 1977 when I came from Baghdad, for a short visit to Wales.

The advert, which was hand written on one of those white small cards said something like 'this first floor one bed flat in Glanmor Road, may seems slightly more expensive than average because it is within a stone's throw from Cwmdonkin Park, and the birth place of the Poet Dylan Thomas'.

It sounded great, a park and a poet. Now I had to break the bad news to my father that I wished to stay in Swansea, probably to study engineering; but the good news, I told him, was that I'll be living close to Dylan Thomas's birth place! My father's reaction was that it would be a very expensive arrangement, and anyway my priority should be to live in a safe place close to the college, not to a poet, and by the way, he added, I have never heard this poet's name.

To cut a long story short, yes, as an 'accidental incomer' I fell in love with Swansea, that 'Ugly, lovely, town' as Dylan put it, and yes, I still haven't used the return part of my airline ticket back to Baghdad. I think it would be rather complicated to argue with Iraqi Airways for a refund after thirty-seven years.

It might have been a landlord in Uplands who introduced me to Dylan Thomas's name, but it was Nigel Jenkins, the Gower poet, and my very close friend, who sadly died this year, who educated me about Dylan's work. Nigel used to read poetry to us in 1978 in a house in Sketty, close to Uplands, where a few refugees from Chile used to live. In 2011 Nigel led a successful campaign to save the well-known Dylan Thomas Centre, which is based in Somerset Place, Swansea from closure. A book entitled *Encounters with Nigel*, put together by the editor of this 'encounters', Jon Gower, will be published shortly by the H'mm Foundation.

Ironically, a few weeks ago I went to Uplands Bookshop, not to look for any accommodation this time, but to collect payment from the sale of my book, *Encounters with R.S.*, which I published last December during the centennial celebrations of his birth, and was edited by John Barnie. The accommodation adverts are still on the window, but no, there were no vacancies in Glanmor Road!

Last week I visited Number 5 Cwmdonkin Drive, my many thanks go to Geoff Haden who restored the Edwardian suburban house, and who classifies himself as being 'mad about Dylan writings'. Geoff manages the day-to-day running of the house together with a small team of volunteers. He is the vice chairman of the Dylan Thomas Society and a founder member of the Dylan Thomas Prize for young writers which is sponsored by Swansea University.

The H'mm Foundation, which has its Head Office on the Swansea University Campus, arranges a poetry reading during the annual Dylan Thomas Prize award ceremony for young writers; among the poets we have invited to read during the ceremony are; Menna Elfyn, Rhian Edwards and Jasmine Donahaye.

I am a businessman, living in Cardiff, with my wife Karen and daughters Lauren and Kathryn. I started the H'mm Foundation over three years ago to build links between the business and arts communities. It has been a creative experience for both, a huge source of inspiration for people in business and a source of additional income for poets.

Introduction: How Green is Our Dylan?

Dafydd Elis-Thomas

We encounter writers as writers only through their texts. Their words are their works. Once writers make the work, those words are on their way to becoming public property by being published in one form or another. That is when they cease to 'belong to the writer', if they ever really did, and become open to interpretations of many different kinds. Poetry as a form of writing exists by being read and listened to, by being heard and interpreted, so I have no hesitation in stating as someone born in Carmarthenshire who has lived with words of Dylan Thomas in his head all his life that his works make him undoubtedly the greenest poet of the 20th century.

Not just because of: 'The force that through the green fuse drives the flower/ Drives my green age;' or 'The secret of the soil grows through the eye,/ And blood jumps in the sun;' or 'Fern Hill' 'Time held me green and dying/ Though I sang in my chains like the sea.' Or 'Over Sir John's hill,/ The hawk on fire hangs still;' but because of the 100 'burning' images of what we used to call 'nature' that I counted once in the 'Author's Prologue' to the *Collected Poems*:

> At God speeded summer's end
> In the torrent salmon sun,
> In my seashaken house
> On a breakneck of rocks
> Tangled with chirrup and fruit,
> Froth, flute, fin and quill
> At wood's dancing hoof,

as the first sentence sings on in exultation at God's creation for thirty lines!

So I was amused to find that campaigners against wind energy were objecting to the decision of Carmarthenshire planners to allow a wind turbine at Llansteffan across the estuary from the Boathouse at Laugharne because it would be 'sited within the vista from Dylan's walk'. This is no doubt what is known as the 'visual amenity' argument wherein the natural world is not lived and felt and smelt and seen as a vibrant process of life and death driven by forces both biological and human, but in the manner of a still life, or a pre-impressionist naturalistic landscape painting as somehow changeless.

I have faith in my reading and interpretation of Dylan Thomas's works that he is the foremost 20th-century poet and writer of community and nature. The 'green fuse' that he felt so keenly pre-dates our current understanding of the terminal threat of climate change. But his name can hardly be conjured up in opposition to renewable energy as a way of supplementing farm incomes in his beloved Carmarthenshire countryside. I'm sure Dylan would share the hawk's eye view from Sir John's hill where a wind turbine is hardly visible through the 'rays of his eyes' compared with 'the small birds of the bay'.

Dafydd Elis-Thomas is the National Assembly Member for the Dwyfor Meirionnydd constituency. He was nominated to the Lords in 1992 and has served as the presiding officer of the National Assembly for three terms.

Encounters with Dylan

A Love for Language

Michael Bogdanov

I am an unashamed Dylan Thomas nut, a collector of first editions of his work, magazines and memorabilia. I have directed *Under Milk Wood* for the stage eleven times, including two productions in German and one in Japanese. It is an irony that *Under Milk Wood* is probably the world's most famous radio play and yet, for many, their knowledge of Thomas's work and reputation rests on a thousand and one stage productions.

I am probably in something of a foreign minority in believing that the Germans have a good sense of humour. Even the German themselves laugh at their reputation – Question: 'What's the shortest book in the world?' Answer: '1001 Years of German Humour.' Certainly my experience of directing *Under Milk Wood* there has never given me grounds to think otherwise, having had to make no concessions whatsoever to culturally comic differences. The German people laugh at the same things, enjoy the same verbal gymnastics, jokes, puns and stage business as any other audience. The problems only begin for Teutonic comic consciousness when the subject moves to 'life' and 'art'. Humour for them plays no part in life or art, humour at that point equates frivolity, lack of seriousness, *oberflächlichkeit* – superficiality. Life and art for the Germans are inseparable and humour belongs to neither. For us when the going gets tough that's when humour kicks in. Satire, irony, ridiculous trouser-dropping absurdity act as cathartic safety valves to stop us getting too worked up about war, poverty, abuse and Tory benefit cuts. A little more Teutonic seriousness would not go amiss.

Herein lies a fundamental difference between the German and the Anglo-Saxon attitude – so near and yet so far. For the funning and the punning British, life and art have absolutely nothing whatsoever to do with each other, but humour is an essential part of both.

And *Under Milk Wood* makes the Germans and the Japanese laugh. A lot. The only difference being that at the conclusion the Germans stand and cheer and the Japanese demonstrate the sound of one hand clapping. And they laugh more than we laugh here in Wales. Why should that be? Why should something that some regard as a piece of parochial, folksy esoteric frivolity strike such a universal chord in foreign parts, in urban communities ostensibly far removed from a small Welsh fishing village? Are we too anxious, too self-critical of ourselves, too familiar with the content? Is *Under Milk Wood* our *Hamlet*, each production measured sceptically against the last? Do The Reverend Ely, Mrs Pugh, Willy Nilly *et al.* measure up to our image of them, to those equivalents of our acquaintance that live around the corner? (Unless that corner is Pontcanna, Cardiff that is.) And then there are those who maintain doggedly that *Under Milk Wood* is a radio play and cannot be staged, ignoring the fact that it is. Constantly. In fifty languages.

Part of the problem lies with the interpretation of the role of First Voice by Thomas himself, which for some has confused the approach to the piece. That mellifluous, honey-tongued, sonorous voice, seductive and seducing – and virtually devoid of the very humour with which Dylan was not only imbued himself as a person but which peppered his prose writings and suffuses *Under Milk Wood* with a warm glow of irreverence. What thrills in the readings of his own and other's poems, here hypnotises. No wonder there was a paucity of giggles, let alone guffaws, to be had on that very first unveiling at the Poetry Centre in New York. It is surprising that Thomas was at all surprised. It was unsurprising, and the recording of this first reading on the Caedmon label has conditioned many a view of the play to this day. How dream like is it, how earthy, how poetic, how funny? How surreal? How real? And it has nothing to do with New Yorkers not understanding the world of Llareggub (see above) and all to do with the Thomas' delivery. What is more the legacy of his dream-like, goose-bumping voice is one bequeathed Richard Burton and then more latterly Tony Hopkins. When a new recording for radio was broadcast by the BBC in 2003 to commemorate fifty years since Dylan's death, the Executive Producers insisted that the original Burton recording from 1954 of the First Voice be used and the new actors tacked on to his interpretation. That did it. No chance. Dream on. Once more unto the voice beautiful, once more, with the oh so many, tongue in the cheek, irreverent references to the idiosyncrasies and vagaries of small town Welsh behaviour, reduced to somnambulistic seriousness. 'Thou shalt not on the wall' should possibly serve as guidance for all aspiring First Voicers. Lighten up. Dylan I'm sure would have had it so.

In 1969, three years after my first *Milk Wood* production in Dublin, I bought a small pub up on the edge of the lonely Mynydd Epynt. Tafarn y Crydd – The Shoemakers Arms – the front room a bar, beer tapped by hand and poured from a jug, empty the Elsan in the stream (Oh dear!) They were all there in that valley, in glorious Technicolor – Ocky Milkman, Dai Bread, Butcher Beynon, Mrs Pugh. On Saturday nights Mrs Ogmore Pritchard (a mountain) would come and haul her second husband (a mole-hill) out by the ears (or ring to accuse us of leading him astray with the devil drink). Organ Morgan played the harmonium in the parlour for the eleven members of the Llandeilo'r Fan Male Voice Choir, and Willy Nilly (Dick the Post actually) would down seventeen pints of flat, warm, thin, Welsh, bitter beer. And laugh? Within five minutes of being back in that pub I laugh like I never laugh anywhere else in the world. These are people who are born together, live together, die together, see each other every day of the week of their ninety-year-old lives and still they find things to laugh about. Folksy they aren't. Hard-living working members of a mountain sheep-farming community they are – battling the elements of centuries to survive. 'The good bad boys from the lonely farms.' And on moonless nights, bible black, flying like black flour, I would stand outside The Shoemakers Arms and look up at The Milky Way and say ' I don't know who's up there and I don't care', and think of *Under Milk Wood*. The spirit of Wales.

My fascination with Dylan did not start with *Milk Wood*, it began much earlier. For my mother, one of thirteen siblings from Neath and born within a month of Dylan, he was a drunkard and a womaniser. For my father he was a supreme wordsmith. My father, a Professor of Modern Languages at Swansea University from 1933-36, possessed a first edition, first impression, of *18 Poems*, one of only 250 copies first printed in 1934, bought when it was first published. As a child he would read me the poems ' The force that through the green fuse drives the flower...' as I listened eagerly (really?), my ten-year-old eyes bright with misunderstanding. 'Tommyrot and twaddle' my mother would announce, adding smugly – 'And anyway, what do you know about communism – you can't even keep your own room tidy'. (Eh?) Years later, in 1958, when I was nineteen, I was to sell that copy, along with a load of early Penguins from my father's collection – numbers 1 to 23 I recall (why on earth did he let me?) – and my prized collection of British stamps – penny blacks and reds, twopenny blues – to fund my gap year in Paris. We're talking serious existentialism here. I blush with shame to remember this crass act of vandalism – selling the books, not the existentialism. Even more so as I later sought out a first edition of *18 Poems* that I could get anywhere near affording.

My love of language is a passion inherited from my father. In pre-revolutionary Russia (Ukraine) before the turn of the century even, in the world in which my father grew up, the word was power. The balladeers, the pamphleteers, the poets, the novelists, the playwrights – those who could read and write held the key to the future. In a world of such devastating illiteracy, they were the truth. They were the word. And the words of Dylan Thomas fascinated him.

My father spoke English with consummate grammatical perfection, as only someone for whom it is not a native language can. And he had the vocabulary to match. Were he alive today he would be shocked to realise how many words that he used in everyday speech have already disappeared or are under threat. But this is the point, language must evolve. We in Wales can relate to that. What price Shakespeare, for example, in 50 to 100 years? With hundreds of words dropping yearly out of use, what will be left of our understanding of his plays in centuries to come if we do not adopt a more radical attitude to these changes? *Beowulf* and Chaucer in translation – why not Shakespeare if it opens up the plays to the vast untapped energies of popular debate?

And Dylan is positively Shakespearean in his verbal constructions and vaulting linguistic combinations. Maybe in fifty years we'll see him, alongside Will.i.am, converted into Americenglish technobabble ad-speak: I look forward to translator convention punch-ups as to what Dylan, Wittgensteinesque, *really* meant.

If my mother belonged to the bunch of local naysayers, the Welsh intelligentsia were no less backward in coming forward to debunk the myth that there was a home grown genius abroad in the Celtic garden. Here's Hywel Williams in *The Guardian* in 2003: –

> *Fifty years ago the roaring boy was coming to the end of his month-long New York drinking session. It was the closest he ever got to an epic achievement. Dylan Thomas in America was doing what he did best – using that booming, fruitily accented voice in order to impersonate the bardic. And business was good as he packed in credulous audiences for his lectures and public readings.*
>
> *Thomas gratified the taste of the States in two ways. First, there was the fake religiosity of his verse – so Parsifal- like in its neo-Christian symbolism. And what he called his 'wordy wounds' were equally Wagnerian in the long-windedness of their bombast about "the celebration of God". For Thomas was a byproduct of the religion of his people, a creed which had long since collapsed into the endless embarrassment of Protestant hymnody. Standing there at the lectern he was just another Welsh preacher concealing the death of the spirit behind the roar of self-love's rhetoric.*
>
> *The cultural quackery worked in another way, too, as Thomas burped his way through Manhattan. He provided his patrons among the American business class with instances of the bogus- Bohemian behaviour regarded by that class as appropriate to a poet: drunken groping and tearful sentiment...*
>
> *Within days the cut-price Dionysiac was dead, having broken his own record for downing double whiskies. While the body was still warm, the cultural trade began of elevating the poetic prankster on to a national pedestal. In death he was acclaimed as a wild Welsh Rimbaud – a comparison he had, preposterously, offered in life. Thomas's resemblance to Rimbaud begins and ends with the fact that after the age of 20 neither produced any work of significance. At least Rim-*

baud turned to gun-running in Abyssinia. Thomas just carried on being a decadent baby in love with his own childishness as he sang in his pram by the sea.

The strict metrical form of Welsh language verse is the ghost that haunts Thomas, but it only existed within his poetry as a kind of obscure intimation of how the real poetic thing might be done. It was the hint of a language lost to him – there in his genes but not in the formless body of his work. The sadness of Thomas the deracinated poet was that he couldn't express himself in English any more than he could in Welsh. So what he ended up writing was really not poetry at all, but rather a kind of demented wordplay – something surely best done with crayons. His poems, in all their babbling weariness, try to recover a baby's view of the world. Which is why reading him is like stumbling into a one-infant workshop in automatic writing. The lines wind their way through abuse of language and end with abuse of self – something which had always been a bit of a Thomas speciality. And along that road to a literary hell paved with squiffy intent, there's abuse of Wales.

The national myth of Thomas has been faithful to the reality of his life in only one respect – its fakery. His survival has essentially been a question of endless productions of Under Milk Wood... For that work has been the single most important anglophone text in providing the English with an essentially treacherous view of Wales. Polly Garter, Organ Morgan and Captain Cat are a colonialist's fantasy of what the natives get up to when Albion's back is turned. And like all such literary exercises of the colonial mind, the object is to demean and control through flattery. Under the folksy quaintness of Milk Wood there lie vicious roots.

The Welsh of the play are irresponsible charmers – impossible but oh-so-loveable. They talk Welsh flannel through their pointed hats while dancing through the Celtic mist. And, having been poetically privileged as artful beauties, *there's a convenient consequence. These people – and what they are supposed to represent – can be twilighted out of existence as they disappear into the mystic west.*

From Richard Burton and Sian Phillips onwards, two generations of Welsh actors have colluded in this sorry little tale by a man who was the literary agent of the colonial condition. Rarely has the national talent for genial submissiveness wound its way quite so stupidly and self-destructively up its own backside.

Phew. Bitter? Moi?

It seems to me – pace the bile – that there is a comprehensive confusion here, a profound inability to separate out the artist from the man – that age old question of how much of an artist goes into the work, how much does one learn of the artist *from* the work. What would we come up with after even a cursory investigation of the 38 plays in the Shakespeare canon? A scholar fluent in Greek, Latin, well-travelled, with a comprehensive knowledge of alchemy, botany, geology, mythology, geography (except that Bohemia has a coastline) intimately acquainted with the ways of the posh boys and girls at the courts of Elizabeth and James. Someone like the Earl of Southampton? (who died in 1604 with fifteen of the greatest plays still unwritten). Francis Bacon? (His extant works are so arse-paralysingly constipated and convoluted that they bear no comparison.) Christopher Marlowe? (He died in a pub punch-up in Deptford early in Shakespeare's career. No he didn't: he escaped to France and spent the next twenty years writing the plays anonymously, sending them back one by one until Shakespeare's death, never reaping the fame, the reward, the money, and forgetting to keep a copy for posterity to vindicate him... ho, ho.) No, you see, the sceptics can't believe that a man educated at best at Stratford Grammar School, who left behind only six signatures, each with a different spelling, who was seemingly preoccupied with nothing more or less than house prices, property speculation and buy-to-rent, could ever possibly have possessed such profound knowledge and philosophical insight into the way the world wags.

By the same token a minute analysis of the poems of DT, without knowing anything of the history of the artist that lay behind them, would never reveal the man or the behaviour. Those meticulous work sheets, a ten-line poem honed and polished gem-like over a period of days, weeks, months – the search for the right word running into hundreds. A womanising, profligate, unwashed roaring boy drunkard? No. At a guess an ascetic, puritanical aesthete (I exaggerate – but not much). And anyway who cares?

The roll-call of artists who have died from their addiction is endless – Janis Joplin, Jimi Hendrix, Michael Jackson, Kurt Cobain, Elvis Presley, Degas, Hemingway, Baudelaire, Dostoyevsky, Cezanne, Bacon, Aldous Huxley, Poe – and that list is just as long as it took me to type. Yet their respective biographies and autobiographies reveal that the majority, as with Thomas, were at their best when they were sober.

The meticulousness of his writing, the hard labour it involved, gives the lie to anyone who thinks that his poetry slithered sideways out of a brain Tasered by alcohol. And far from not writing anything of worth after the age of twenty some of the greatest poems were penned in the latter phase of his life, including what now must be the most quoted poem in the world – 'Do not go gentle into that good night'. Avid cricket fan Thomas would have delighted in the headline to the third Ashes Test in Australia last winter when bad light cheated England of a win: 'Rage Against the Dying of the Light'.

The only puzzle, as Jeff Towns articulated, is at what point did the transition from the doggerel-strewn jokey Juvenilia of *The Swansea Grammar School Magazine* turn a year or so later into the astonishing 'I see the boys of summer in their ruin', 'Especially when the October wind', 'Light breaks where no light shines' etc. of the *18 Poems* that bought me a train and a boat ride to Paris and my first adventures in the skin trade (Scandinavian). That's a puzzle to rival who wrote Shakespeare (answers on a Boathouse postcard please) but so far no relative or upholder of a challenger, the model of Puritan purse-lipped sobriety, has stepped forward to claim Dylan's crown. Luckily, unlike Shakespeare, there's too much evidence.

Cucumber and Hooves

Kaite O'Reilly

I knew of him first as the bad man who 'turned' a good Irishwoman the way a drop of lemon will turn fresh milk sour for the making of soda bread. She had been good, and then she was spoiled, a chemical reaction as swift and irreversible as curdling.

Not that she was all that innocent or God-fearing to begin with, according to Aunty Kathleen. She was from *those* Macnamaras, notorious, what with all them artists and bohemians and the knack for swimming in the nuddy and posing the same way, too, in the buff, imagine! I couldn't. Being in the nuddy was something you did when totally alone and with the stiff key turned in the lock, not in front of a photographer out in a field with an armful of hay, balanced one-footed on the seat of a threshing machine.

And anyways, them Macnamaras were Anglo-Irish *prods*, not the real stuff from Country Clare going back to the children of Caisin from the second century AD. She was London-Irish, and worse, London-Anglo-Irish, and even better-worse a godless, drinking, smoking, cursing, brawling adulteress, neglecter of children. That Caitlin Thomas *nee* Macnamara was never a true Irishwoman and never a good one to begin with. Maybe it was she who was the sour one; the citric acid turning that weak coddled Welshman into a soak and a corpse.

*

My introduction to the Dylan Thomas mythology was Irish and Caitlin-centric. There was little reference to his work and reputation, just sighs and tut-tuts over the endless drinking and terrible waste. This was in Ireland after all, and the curse of the nation was, and remains, drink.

Caitlin Thomas was a warning against the pull of the literary life, a precautionary tale of too much passion and poverty mixed with the hard stuff. Maybe she became an amulet against my possible future because we shared a first name and I was polishing up the reputation of being a little wild, myself. 'You hold the bone in your mouth and the dogs'll come running after it,' my Mother told me endlessly in my teens. 'You want to keep yourself *nice*.'

I resisted, for I knew it was the not-nice girls who were interesting and going places. Nice girls spent too much time grooming themselves and fretting about what everyone thought. Nice girls were boring and put themselves last. I had hunger and appetite and the means to satisfy myself. My icons were broken, productive, angry women: the Frida Kahlos, the Martha Gellhorns, the Jean Rhyses, the Tina Modottis. I wasn't sure about Caitlin Thomas. Like Zelda Fitzgerald, she seemed an extraordinary force of nature thwarted by her man and their inebriate lifestyle.

'You don't want to end up like Dylan Thomas's wife,' I was warned more than a few times when moving to Cardiff in my twenties. 'You be careful of them men in Wales, especially them that fancy themselves artistic, and especially, God help us, poetic.' The warning was completed with a roll of the eyes and a knuckle-dance of the crucifix across the face and clavicles.

We knew all about literary ambitions in Dublin. You couldn't pass along Grafton Street without tripping over Roddy Doyle selling his self-published chronicle of Barrytown out of a cardboard suitcase at his feet. But he was the exception, the go-getter, not the tavern talker, the public house poet. The city was full of wagging jaws and stories spun from the roasted barley of St James's Gate. 'And bills unpaid and children going to bed hungry, their belly thinking their throat's been slit. You don't want a blatherer,' my Mother advised me. 'If you have to have a man, be sure he's a doer and not just a talker. Fine words never buttered any parsnips – so you've been warned.'

I *had* been warned and therefore suspicious of any man with a lyrical phrase in his mouth and designs on my body. As I had literary pretensions myself, I needed to be the antithesis of a 'wife'. I had to be on guard, otherwise like the Pop Art feminist cartoons of the eighties, I'd sink into his arms and end up with my arms in the sink, a litter of ankle-biters crowding my DMs, art and creativity flown out the window.

I only had to look at the domestic misery of the Thomases in the mid-1940s to see where it could all end: the begging letters, the neglect of their children for a gaudy night-out, a seemingly bleak existence (for Caitlin at least) carried out in asbestos-filled hovels with no amenities. I already knew of the eighteen Manhattan whiskeys chased down one after the other, allegedly causing the greatest 'insult' to that astonishing brain. I might not have read one word of his poems at the time, but I knew his weakness, and I feared and distained it.

Dylan Thomas was what my Mother, a barmaid, would call a messy drunk. In our household it didn't matter how much you drank as long as you could maintain your dignity through correct pronunciation of difficult words whilst remaining conscious in an upright stance. We were started young, a ball of Irish in a thimble when we had visitors over from home. To hog the bottle and drink so much as to become soft-mouthed and bladdered was frowned upon. To drink to the point of extinction was inexcusably amateur. So not only was Thomas a bad man who may or may not have turned a good Irishwoman to the wrong, he was a sloppy drinker, another in the hopeless pantheon of squandered genius.

Moving to Wales suddenly brought the mythology up close and alive. Acquaintances spoke of Caitlin and Dylan Thomas as though gossiping about their neighbours, which in some cases they had been. Someone's Nan had lived on Cwmdonkin Drive in Swansea and gone to school with Dylan's sister Nancy, an Uncle had stood him and George Orwell a drink in the Wheatsheaf in Fitzrovia. Others had family that knew her from The Dolau Inn in Newquay, or had talked lambing with him and Tommy Herbert the vet in the Central Hotel in Llanon.

In all this interaction, whether in Ireland, England, or Wales, the writing never figured. My new Welsh friends didn't quote this Thomas the way they did RS, memorably bursting into proclamations prompted by the landscape or tractors or the elusive nature of God. How extraordinary then to finally, and late in the day, encounter some of Dylan's words. It was a rehearsed reading in Sheffield, and I was a last minute replacement. I hadn't the chance to prepare or even read the text in advance. I was thrust into a seat on stage and given someone else's script, the parts to be read marked in yellow highlighter. Various characters. All women. The lights in the auditorium dimmed and my life changed.

I don't care if he's common... as long as he's all cucumber and hooves.

The yearning innocent sauce of it. Desire, yielding and assertive, viscerally pungent yet softened by inexperience. Even the name Gossamer Beynon was enough to send me into a rapture of consonants and vowels.

I sat on stage mesmerised by the textures of voices in the air and playing on the bones of my inner ear: that opening dark invocation of dreams and memory, visions and death. I closed my eyes to savour a sudden soaring lyricism like the song of a lark. Sentences lengthened into great waves like the roiling sea behind the eyelids of the sleepers and around the slumbering town. Mid-performance I truly understood the definition of incantation – '*a ritual recitation of verbal charms or spells to produce a magic effect*' – and staggered away, intoxicated.

Here was someone as obsessed with words as Joyce, the same riotous pleasure in sounds and tempo-rhythm, multiple meanings and puns, but less esoteric. Dylan Thomas's ravishing accessibility in *Under Milk Wood* had the sexy, sly, self-deprecating wryness of a John Donne seduction poem, an unashamed wide-eyed wonder at existence crossed with a crowd-pleasing wink to the music hall gallery. I loved it. Reared on Synge, I knew that each speech in a good play '*should be as fully flavoured as a nut or apple.*' In Thomas's play for voices, Milk Wood was clearly an orchard.

What followed for this atheist was something like a religious conversion. I was able to pull away from under the yoke of the four sacred cows of Irish culture: Yeats, Joyce, Beckett, and Synge. I had assumed my bowed genuflection was mandatory. Somehow, after experiencing this play for voices, I was free to reinvent my relationship to language, guided by the excesses and restraints of this new master craftsman. As a playwright I had always been annoyed how critics attributed the rhythms and patterns of my dialogue, inherited from my charismatic, storytelling parents, to this linguistic gang of four. Now, it was different. As an artist I stood apart.

Discovering Dylan Thomas's skill with language, characterisation, and metaphor in *Under Milk Wood* somehow liberated me from my own national writers. I felt an affinity with the timbre of his work, but no competition or responsibility. I understand now of course the irony of the situation. My Welsh peers were as bowed down under the weighty legacy of Dylan Thomas as I was by Beckett and Joyce. A poet from Carmarthen once told me if he glanced askance into the mirror, Dylan's sulky pout appeared fleetingly over his shoulder. An emerging playwright from Mountain Ash sent an email after listening to the 1954 Richard Burton recording saying 'WHY EVEN BOTHER AFTER THAT????!!!!!' My reply was succinct: 'Because it's not a contest. He's a master to learn from, not a bloody rival.'

The spirit is in the detail, the cadence, the composition. He crafts astonishing and memorable characters from words, textures, and sensations, not back-story or psychology, that awkward phrase 'narratology.' All I need to know about the world of the play and its inhabitants is rendered in the dialogue, a surprising or complicit juxtaposition (cucumber and hooves) that exposes the inner life, dreams, and aspirations. And not a bit of it po-faced, arrogant, or worthy. It's the flash of brilliance of the kingfisher diving into a river, not the self-regarding preen of the peacock displaying his gorgeous tail.

*

And then years passed and I moved to west Wales, a mile or so from Newquay, the fabled study for Llareggub. My favourite spot in spring is on Llanina Point, tucked in behind St Ina's Church, out of the wind and surrounded by bluebells. The fierce storms early in 2014 challenged an already eroded coastline. Rumour has it that a village here fell into the sea, homes, church, and graveyard, drowned by the waves. The current church is the third on the spot, built in the 1850s from the remnants of shipwrecks and the previous church. One of my favourite hidey-holes, John Ackerman maintains, was the literal inspiration for Captain Cat's dead dears.

Not that all of the graves are – or were – inhabited. I often think of the sailors lost at sea or in foreign parts, those whose bodies were never returned to grace the Welsh graves teetering on the edge of the cliff. It has a poignant poetry for me as I pass between the headstones, thinking of the disembodied voices of Thomas's sailors here double-drowned, once in reality and once symbolically, their marked but empty graves tumbling into the waves.

And here suddenly it all comes together on my local walk. Across from the graveyard is the recent reproduction of the sixteenth-century mansion Plas Llanina. In its grounds and parallel with St Ina are the ruins of its old family chapel, used as a studio by Augustus John, deflowerer or rapist of Caitlin, depending on the account (the nonchalance of this fact has always deeply troubled me). It was Augustus John who first brought Dylan Thomas here to seek a patron in Lord Howard de Waldon, and, indeed, it was this old goat of an artist who introduced the couple.

A little further along the walled garden of Plas Llanina with its ragged raw lip falling to the sea is where Dylan occasionally wrote, looking across to the beach where Caitlin famously bathed. Several hundred metres up the road, past the Llanina woods, is where Majoda once stood, a wooden shack with no running water, plumbed gas or electricity. There the Thomases spent a difficult, but artistically productive year, where *Under Milk Wood* was started, and various major long poems completed. It overlooked Cardigan Bay and had a field up front, rented by de Waldon to a farmer who grazed cows there. This provided part of the inspiration for the title of the play, David N. Thomas believes, along with New Quay's fame for abundant hazel copses and 'their crops of milky nuts' as *The Welsh Gazette* coined it.

I'm not a fan of the official 'Dylan Thomas Trail', finding the commemorative plaques dotted about on walls and front doors confusing and uninformative. Perhaps it's the disturbingly blue mottled chubby-cheeked likeness of the young poet on the plaques that troubles me so, or the half-hearted attempt to spin some kind of cheap literary tourism in the place where I live. It reminds me of South Tyneside's embarrassing attempt to rebrand the area 'Catherine Cookson Country'.

At least we're currently spared Polly Garter's Pantry, or Organ Morgan's General Store, or Myfanwy Price Is Right Famous Pound Shop, but perhaps with this year's centenary it's only a matter of time. Better to follow David N. Thomas's guides in his books or website, enjoying a stretch of the legs along this glorious stretch of coast.

*

And here is where my trail ends, caught up in the reimagining and repackaging of Caitlin and Dylan.

I entered a story of them through stories of my own family and our dialogue. Somehow, through the chance and coincidence of living, narrative strands have crossed and interwoven, occasionally running opposite, occasionally parallel.

My Aunty Kathleen is long dead, joining the Corcorans and the Carrs in the Balbriggan graveyard and now my parents, too, are gone, though their words play through my head every day. And perhaps that is all we have – the stroke of words across the consciousness, language glancing like headlights across the night-time bedroom ceiling. We are all like Dylan's sleepers, a beam of illumination, then gone.

Like a Fiery Chaffinch:
Dylan Thomas & Nature

Horatio Clare

Most British people love to go to Italy, for a holiday; for sun, art, religion, vino rosso della casa. Those of us whose souls will ever sing for a cypress morning, for the dark sentinels lining a smiling land – bonjourno to the mezzogiorno! – we happy many, we race of nature-lovers, we welcome the land beyond the Alps with delight. And here is that great poet of nature whose centenary we salute in this his springing anniversary year, 2014. Dylan Thomas writes:

> In a shuttered room I roast
> Like a pumpkin in a serra
> And the sun like buttered toast
> Drips upon the classic terra

Sharing with him a childhood in Wales, and visits to Florence – we went by coach via London – I recognise him and his worlds like a boy I met once, a dream I had once, the dream of childhood in Wales. As for Italy, 'sun like buttered toast' is exactly right. My brother, then eight, was once overheard as he was strolling, head down, around the pool at the villa above Florence (then an exquisite Medici dilapidation) where we stayed, billeted with English students who were trading labour for shelter with the laughing Baron, Amerigo Franchetti of the Torre di Bellosguardo – who has since made the Torre the city's best hotel, with that fine pool overlooking a divine view of the Duomo, the Arno and the rest – calling, gently, 'Here Toss! Here Toss! Good boy...' Young Alexander had only been separated from his hound and the Cwmdu valley for a week.

The place we never wanted to leave was Pembrokeshire, and the dogs came too. Every year the last week in August or sometimes the first of September, we spent at Little Haven, guests of my mother's former teachers. They kept Lantern Cottage on Walton Hill for the old gels. The very poorest of the gels and their families (it was a school for missionaries' daughters, and outstanding) were then very rich for a short span. The Ladies of Little Haven, as they were known, insisted on sums no greater than thirty pounds. My mother wrote embarrassed and grateful cheques. The munificence of the west Wales coast is beyond compare, almost beyond capture in words. I have my sacred places; we all do. Dylan's were further south, up-channel, but this could be any good headland between Llantwit and Aberdaron:

> *Even on the calmest day a wind blew along the Worm. At the end of the humped and serpentine body, more gulls than I had ever seen before cried over their new dead and the droppings of ages. On the point, the sound of my quiet voice was scooped and magnified into a hollow shout, as though the wind around me had made a shell or cave, with blue intangible roof and sides, as tall and wide as all the arched sky, and the flapping gulls were made thunderous.*[1]

I had to write something once about summer in novels in what they are pleased to call English Literature and could make no comment about this: I said it was beyond criticism, mighty music, and so it is. We note the exactitude, which you will find in everyone from Mabey to Macfarlane, Perrin to Jeffries, H.E. Bates and BB; from Thoreau, indeed, to Wordsworth. We mark the audible power of the writing, note the way the visual is run on one axis reaching out from us, beyond the gulls, into the blue distance, while the descriptions of sound rise above us, adding the third and fourth dimension. We gather the speaker moves from the base of the peninsula to the tip, there is a rush-forward in the feel of it, though there are no mentions of forward motion after 'a wind blew along the Worm', only 'flapping gulls' going up and down. We feel thrown movement in 'scooped and magnified', but the propellant charge of the lines is an alchemy of suggestion and observation. And the speaker speaks. This is not always someone who falls silent in the face of natural marvel. This is someone who talks across the miracle, and writes across it too. See him in carving words on benches in Cwmdonkin Park? He is still doing it, in his thousands.

Being children of agricultural Wales, if we might euphemise hill farming thus, rather than sons of the industrial coast, suburban Swansea, hailing from what he describes as 'outside, a strange Wales, of choirs and sheep and story-book tall hats' Alexander and I knew only a depopulated variant of Dylan's Cwmdonkin Park. Ours was Park Farm in Llangattock, a wilderness beyond the playground fences of fallen trees, Rhododendrons, misdeeds, hacked confessions of want in bleeding bark and, once, the smeared turds of Jason Bird, a big BMX boy in the year above who had defied lavatory paper. There were no Cwmdonkin nannies, pushing prams, girls or many other boys. There was no one, and neither was there anyone on our hill, save the walkers on bank holidays who Toss bit, and our neighbours cursing their dogs on the skyline. Our encounters with nature were therefore enormous: the buzzards and crows were all our peers. Dylan's were no less impressing, perhaps much more so, for his nature, mixed with town, required and supplied imagination. He was 'hunter and herdsman'. He 'ran like a billy goat over the grass'. He lit fires in the bushes and had fights in the bandstand, and on 'the long splendid shore' ('There was another world,' he writes, almost breathlessly), he went to 'remember adventures and make more to remember'.

Being But Men

Being but men, we walked into the trees
Afraid, letting our syllables be soft
For fear of waking the rooks,
For fear of coming
Noiselessly into a world of wings and cries.

If we were children we might climb,
Catch the rooks sleeping, and break no twig,
And, after the soft ascent,
Thrust out our heads above the branches

To wonder at the unfailing stars.

Out of confusion, as the way is,
And the wonder, that man knows,
Out of the chaos would come bliss.

That, then, is loveliness, we said,
Children in wonder watching the stars,
Is the aim and the end.

Being but men, we walked into the trees.

This is as close to Shakespearean beauty and truth as many writers counted in the canon of 'English Literature', and so far as we know any outside it, have come. And it is only a nature poem, on one level.

We went our ways – my brother to Aberystwyth, New York and London. Me, the *Mid Devon Gazette*, the *Western Mail*, *The Richmond and Twickenham Times*, *The Newcastle Chronicle and Journal*, one short and embarrassing shift on the *Nottingham Evening Post*, and thence The Chelsea Potter, 119 King's Road, Chelsea, and Broadcasting House, London W1A 1AA. There in disused studio B10 a smoking room had been established, fifty feet underground, and there we smoked. There was a photo on the wall of Dylan in the same studio when it was working, reading with Richard Burton and smoking. Not until I began work on this essay did I notice how closely my life, if only circumstantially and to this point, echoes his. Sir Paul Schofield, Felicity Kendal, Sam West, Georgia Mackenzie, Richard 'Welsh' Coyle – I worked with great actors there too. Dylan was on the *Swansea Evening Post*, and then in London, and then in Broadcasting House, broadly.

The parlour scene in *A Portrait of the Artist as a Young Dog*, the meeting of the literary society, when he describes a version of himself aiming to move to London and hoping vaguely to live on women: I adore that story, likewise the gilded catalogue, that magnificent illuminated bestiary with which he launches *Under Milk Wood*. He writes of men and women like a nature writer of genius writing about nature. There was no division between 'the other world' of the strands of the Severn Sea and Cwmdonkin Park, the trimmed and litter-binned outpost of nature at the end of his road. They were one. Men and women are animals; cities are only projections of nature (he writes 'sea town' and 'sea-town' often, yoking them together), coronets on the dolphin land, and Dylan rushes the lot of it, with his firey trumpets. Hence 'A Refusal to Mourn the Death, by Fire, of a Child in London':

> Never until the mankind making
> Bird beast and flower
> Fathering and all humbling darkness
> Tells with silence the last light breaking
> And the still hour
> Is come of the sea tumbling in harness
>
> And I must enter again the round
> Zion of the water bead
> And the synagogue of the ear of corn
> Shall I let pray the shadow of a sound
> Or sow my salt seed
> In the least valley of sackcloth to mourn
>
> The majesty and burning of the child's death.
> I shall not murder
> The mankind of her going with a grave truth
> Nor blaspheme down the stations of the breath
> With any further
> Elegy of innocence and youth.
>
> Deep with the first dead lies London's daughter,
> Robed in the long friends,
> The grains beyond age, the dark veins of her mother,
> Secret by the unmourning water
> Of the riding Thames.
> After the first death, there is no other.

There are memories of Coleridge in this, and Shelley, another great sympathetic sufferer, who I think must be Thomas' closest friend in the Empyreal Bar where all the poets drink and compose away eternity. Prose writers, sadly, are not admitted to that celestial establishment where, as Bruce Robinson put it, Keats will be buying the drinks. We have to make do with a restaurant. But it's the same hotel.

In 1997, vaguely on the run from Mid Devon, I walked into the Hotel Chelsea and asked Stanley Bird for a room, explaining that I was a writer from Wales. (If you have to announce yourself, Thomas might have smiled...) He looked you up and down like a buzzard sizing a gizzard and committed me to an extraordinary bedroom suite: huge, dark-wooded with a bath like a squash court for tuppence and 59 bucks or something. I lay in that bath reading Shelley's translations of the Greeks on love. No more now than then could I really break the Symposium down for you, except the scene where they are all hungover except Socrates.

Perhaps you could write about more than the Chelsea itself, or New York or love and sex there; perhaps – but not me. Certainly even scrawled pastiches of the novels, plays, poems and that Cohen song were beyond me. Instead I attended the final of a nationwide dance competition in the Copacabana that night, with Abigail, the most beautiful receptionist at the Paramount Hotel. An actress, Abigail with her ravenwing hair and exquisitely cut, pale face, dark luminous eyes and perfect pallor was moonlighting as a featured dancer in the national Macarena Contest. Her name was Walker until she got fed up of me soiling her flat in Queens whereupon it was Giordano, and her family were in Chicago. Thomas, meanwhile:

'The cockroaches have teeth,' he writes. 'I've just seen the gates of hell', he said, later, after too much booze. A biographer, Paul Ferris: 'On Sunday there was a matinee performance of Milk Wood, reportedly the best of the four given in New York. At a party afterwards Thomas gulped whisky and disappeared upstairs with a woman.'

The wild life of the Five Boros is dazzling to a boy from the hills of south Wales who really knows only hills, or seas, and little houses. Abigail was appearing in an off-Broadway play. Her director/playwright loved her. Warren hated me on sight. It ended badly at the cast party, though we were destined to meet one more time.

Meanwhile, Thomas: 'The dollar-mad nightingale' in his own phrase, taken with 'naked women in wet mackintoshes' as cited in *Dylan Thomas: Poet of His People* by Andrew Sinclair, (Michael Joseph, London 1975) eventually went home, finally, an 'embalmed body, 'sodden, limp from indistinguishable hangovers', half killed by the care of his friends' in Thomas's words and Sinclair's judgment. More than any other writer he seems to outlive, surround and curate his death. Or perhaps it is that way with all of them if you read them long. Certainly it – death – is among all their best subjects.

'Life writing', I sometimes think could well be entitled 'Death writing'. Half the plot is determined by dead people; the impulse to tell and record life exists under and thanks to the sharp hands of the old scytheman, in autobiography and biography defiance and hope are all, and 'life writing' has to end somewhere, after all. Dylan does a lot of it; he is perhaps the superlative practitioner of life-writing-with-a-nature-slant. (And who does not, honestly, Wayne Rooney and Jordan excepted, include some nature in their best-selling life-writing?) Certainly, even against Alistair Cooke and the best of our own correspondents, I think he fights for the honours for life-writing for broadcast.

Should any hypothesise I hyperbolise: in late May 1961 a young South African, Stephanie Kemp, wrote her name in her new hardback copy of *Quite Early One Morning – Broadcasts by Dylan Thomas* published by J M Dent & Sons Ltd of Bedford Street, London, preface by Aneirin Talfan Davies of Wales Region, BBC. The book passed to her boyfriend, the Cape Town student and journalist John Clare, a future BBC reporter and broadcaster, who kept it through the seventies and the eighties when he briefly lived with Stephanie again, then had it in his flat near hers, in Tufnell Park, and kept it for many years afterwards until he ill-advisedly lent it to one of his sons in the late nineties. I have had it since 1997 at least. In Shadwell in 1999 I vowed never to part with it. The cover shows D. Thomas in a black polo-neck, looking clean, smart, young, sober and angelically focused on the script in front of him: a magnificent prospect, balm to any producer's programme-day heart! Behind him, through the glass, you can see that man in a suit. It is our smoking room, Studio B10, and work is about to commence. In Tom Stoppard's dialogue of *Shakespeare in Love*, the producer will shortly see, and we will hear, as Ben Affleck's Mercutio tells Geoffrey Rush, 'how genius creates a legend'.

I am not proud of this bit. The last time I saw Abigail was the morning after the cast party when she returned to her flat to find me in her stairwell – it had been a long, blizzard-ridden night, and a cold trek for a broke drunk from Manhattan – sullenly insisting on my grandmother's small suitcase, in which all my worldlies, including my passport. Abigail was escorted by a muscular, handsome young man, a bouncer from the Paramount, who was also perhaps not unwitting of her family in Chicago. I did not fight him; though D. Thomas, in my state then, may have.

Instead, as the taxi did a u-turn, I rolled down the window of the black sedan and shouted across the quiet Queens' street something I regret, twice, and her name. In the airport at the gate I learned that Abigail or someone had photocopied my passport and passed it to the authorities. Two NYPD patrolmen looked me up and down almost wistfully. I was polite – and pretty jacked up on dog anaesthetic, residual heroin, cannabis and vodka, Hunter style. The issue and its right upshot seemed to be in swing when the Virgin Atlantic check-in person said her airline would be happy to fly the passenger. There was a pause. I added 'Or we could call the British Embassy?'

One patrolman said, 'Where are you going?'

'Home,' I said.

'When were you planning to come back?' He slapped my passport rapidly on his fist.

'Here? I'm not. Not for a while.'

'Good. Ok. Do that.'

And so I was free to fly home and turn myself in to Mid Devon, which I duly did. But I was much younger then than Thomas was on his last trip and I should not like to try anything like it now.

Quite Early One Morning

*Quite early one morning in the winter in Wales, by the sea
that was lying down still and green as grass after a night of
tar-black howling and rolling, I went out of the house, where
I had come for a cold unseasonable holiday, to see if it was
raining still, if the outhouse had been blow away, potatoes,
shears, rat-killer, shrimp nets, and tins of rusty nails aloft on
the wind, and if all the cliffs were left. It had been such a fe-
rocious night that someone in the smoky ship-pictured bar
had said he could feel his tombstone shaking, even though
he was not dead, or at least was moving; but the morning
shone as clear and calm as one always imagines tomorrow
will shine.*

*The sun lit the sea town, not as a whole – from top-most
down – reproving zinc-roofed chapel to empty-but-for rats-
and-whispers grey warehouse on the harbour, but in separate
bright pieces. There, the quay shouldering out, no one on it
but gulls and the capstans like small men in tubular trousers.
Here the roof of the police station, black as a helmet, dry as
a summons, sober as Sunday. There, the splashed church,
with a cloud in the shape of a bell poised above it, ready to
drift and ring. Here the chimneys of the pink-washed pub,
the pub that was waiting for Saturday night as an over-jolly
girl waits for sailors.*

The town was not yet awake...

That flat in Shadwell was sixty a week, there were three of us, and
all our neighbours were Bangladeshi. There was a Hawksmoor church
out the back, St George in the East, and I was working at the bottom of
BBC Radio. I went to get my ears syringed and wrote my first half-
decent non-juvenile poem about it, which I have since lost. It is on a
hard drive which is hidden in the then-dry bilges of a river cruiser which
was moored at Lisson Grove. My room was a warm box and Stephanie
Kemp's copy of *Quite Early One Morning* never looked better than

under my bedside light. I don't know how many times I read those two paragraphs then, as the capstans like small men in tubular trousers were carved into my wrting heart. Now, years later, new sounds of his make pictures to inscribe with them.

> All the moon long I herd, blessed among stables,
> Nightjars flying with the ricks.
>
> Time held me green and dying
> Though I sang in my chains like the sea.

There are many of us, these days, who are called Nature Writers, and many more Life Writers, and there are poets. I know he has the better of each of these forms, as none of us do today. Happy birthday Mr Thomas. Don't be a stranger now...

1: From the short story 'Who Do You Wish was with Us?'

Smuthound:
Obscenity and Dysfunction in the Short Stories of Dylan Thomas

Rachel Trezise

My rendezvous-by-proxy with the Kardomah boy, this powwow in particular at any rate, happened late in a life soused by encounters with Dylan Thomas and followed a fracas with a retired public school teacher early in February 2007 on the patio of Dylan's former Boathouse. I'd been booked for an event chaired by Alun Gibbard, probably a reading and short Q&A, having won the inaugural Dylan Thomas Prize five months earlier. It clashed with Wales' opening Six Nations match against Ireland, a cold Sunday afternoon. The small audience waiting for us at the picnic tables, cream teas steaming against the winter sunshine, were middle-aged; a pair of couples from Pontardawe, (the alpha-female had heard me interviewed on *Woman's Hour* while she ironed her son-in-law's shirts), and a couple from St Albans, Hertfordshire, English teachers both, holidaying in inimitable Laugharne. Whatever experience I had as a writer at that point intuited me to apologise beforehand for the strong language in the story I was about to read, but I'd learn that afternoon that admitting a flaw to a live audience is a little like opening a vial of blood under the nostrils of an insatiable predator. The male teacher from the Home Counties became increasingly aggravated throughout the story, sighing noisily and muttering at mentions of the words 'tits' 'AIDS' and 'paedophile'. When I stopped reading he stood to tell the small gathering on the patio how very appalled he was. He'd been expecting a 'quiet afternoon, a cultural experience, prose more akin to Dylan Thomas himself'. Gibbard tried to guide the commotion into a rational discussion, asking me if I thought contemporary literature was deliberately trying to overstep the mark. My answer, that contemporary literature seemingly hadn't got anywhere near the 'mark' aggravated the retired teacher anew. He began on a fresh rant, something about 'dysfunction' and 'standards', his face turning crimson, until the alpha-female from Pontardawe decided to stand herself and shout him down. 'For God's sake man,' she pointed at the back door of the Boathouse, 'did you pay any attention at all to the exhibition? Dylan Thomas has been dead for fifty years.'

My understanding of Thomas's work at that instant was contemptible. My trajectory from average Treorchy Comprehensive School pupil to published and award winning writer was unorthodox, fuelled by rock lyrics rather than poetry, fanzine writing rather than literary competitions and determination rather than expertise. If I'd read anything at all before embarking on my debut novel it was African-American women: Maya Angelou, Toni Morrison, Alice Walker, as far away from white Welsh men as it was possible to get in the English language. Of course I knew of *Under Milk Wood*; I'd read the first three pages of the script with an enthusiastic supply teacher as a thirteen-year-old and been mystified by her irrepressible adoration for it. Too young perhaps to note the cutting wit of the First Voice, too bashful to appreciate the biting humour in the naming of characters like Organ Morgan, Gossamer Beynon, Bessie Bighead and Nogood Boyo. I remember thinking it rambling and dull, parochial, and, strangest of all, a little bit 'churchy'. Ditto *A Child's Christmas in Wales* which seemed to make an appearance every December, verbose with images of snow and archaic Christmas gifts like 'many-coloured jelly babies' 'tin soldiers' and picture-less books about small boys who drowned skating on Farmer Giles' frozen pond. 'Or I would go out, my bright new boots squeaking, into the white world, on to the seaward hill, to call on Jim and Dan and Jack and to pad through the still streets, leaving huge deep footprints on the hidden pavements.' A world away from my rain-spattered Rhondda Valley Barbie-doll and poverty-themed Christmas's of the 1980s. I couldn't have known that the piece was a combination of two reminiscences, both deliberately laced with nostalgia in order to please the producers at BBC Wales and, across the pond, the editor at *Harper's Bazaar*, for money to keep the wolves from the door.

Because of the high regard with which *A Child's Christmas in Wales* was and is still held, I presumed that it was one of Thomas' greatest works, in prose form at least; the epitome of his *oeuvre*. Like Richard

Llewellyn's *How Green was my Valley*, which I had indeed read, I came to think of Dylan Thomas's work as sentimental and bathetic, depicting life in south Wales as pacific and idyllic, so that even when Meic Stephens, tutoring me at the former University of Glamorgan on a module called 'The Short Story' had urged the Welsh students in the class to scrutinise the work of Welsh writers, Thomas in particular, I purposely avoided it. And, because of these misconceptions, I fully accepted that the retired teacher from Hertfordshire had come to the Boathouse in Laugharne expecting something less dysfunctional, less contemporary and less honest, something that slipped a little easier down the throat with the buttered scone and sugary tea. I had knowingly gone out of my way to evade Welsh literary tradition, Welsh mysticism and romanticism, and written with a naïve voice that came spontaneously from me, and by extension, the anglicised Welsh valleys. Whoever'd booked me to read at the Boathouse had made a dire mistake. This was tourist board Wales; somewhere to stop and nibble at light refreshments between a ride on a steam train and a hike to a castle ruins. Holidaymakers from the Home Counties had no regard for the reality of the valleys, sick and withering still at the collapse of the coal industry.

It was five or six weeks later when I found myself, stranded at Newark airport, my flight to Austin, Texas delayed by five hours, the only book in my hand luggage the *Collected Stories of Dylan Thomas*. It had been a gift from the Dylan Thomas Prize, propped on the bedside in the hotel rooms of the shortlisted authors. I'd brought it to the US out of gratitude. I supposed I might skim it lightly before visiting the Dylan Thomas collection at the Harry Ransom Centre. Stubborn as ever, I had no intention of actually reading it. And yet there I was, one page in and engrossed by a claim in Leslie Norris' introduction that Thomas's editor refused his early stories thinking them 'obscene'. Obscene? Really? So I read 'The Dress', a story about an escaped madman, Jack, imprisoned for cutting his wife's lips off 'because she smiled at other men'. Jack has a dream in which sleep appears as a girl in a flowered dress. The dream comes true when Jack breaks into the house of a young woman in a floral dress and she lets him sleep with his head in her lap.

Then I read 'The Burning Baby', a story about a preacher called 'Rhys Rhys.' (There's one of those satirical Welsh character names again; a character in the story I'd read at the Boathouse was called 'Rhys Davies John Davies'.) Rhys Rhys has an incestuous relationship with his daughter. When she gives birth to their child he sets fire to it in order to rid the earth of the fruit of a 'foul womb.' Dysfunctional much? I'd learn later that novelist Glyn Jones had given Dylan Thomas the idea for the story when he told him about physician William Price, an eccentric who burned the body of his dead, illegitimate son on a hill in Llantrisant in 1884, having long been an advocate of cremation and paving the way for its legalisation in 1902. At the time I was stunned at how 'churchy' the story wasn't. The whole thing pointed at the dangers of religious hypocrisy. I remember looking up at a Bruce Springsteen poster on the airport wall and marvelling at how wrong Reagan's 1984 presidential campaign had been to use 'Born in the USA' to champion its right wing policies. Springsteen fans knew the song had been written to confront the legacy of Vietnam.

Even some of the subsequent stories in *Portrait of the Artist as A Young Dog*, Thomas's beloved autobiographical collection of stories about youth and young adulthood in Swansea, structurally his strongest prose work, address macabre and foreboding themes. In particular, 'Just Like Little Dogs' in which Tom and Walter meet Norma and Doris, pair off, copulate in a park, change partners, become pregnant and remain unaware of the identity of the babies' father, and 'Old Garbo' in which Freddie Farr, senior reporter at the *Tawe News* takes a budding reporter on a crawl through the seedy docks pubs and Mrs Prothero, 'Old Garbo', after collecting a hat full of money to fund her dead daughter's funeral, commits suicide because of course her daughter isn't really dead and she's spent all the money on booze.

Thomas was well aware his stories contained the power to offend. Publishing houses rejected them time and again, editors describing them as 'horrible' 'disgusting' and a 'welter of pornographic filth'. For a time he tried to placate everybody substituting stories deemed 'vulgar' for 'cleaner' autobiographical fables about his grandparents or neighbours. What would our retired teacher from Hertfordshire think of Dylan

Thomas if he knew Thomas had once written these words to Wyn Henderson, acting as his agent: 'Thank you for working [on] the stories, I do hope you succeed in making the meanies realise I'm not a smuthound.'

Intriguing though it was, the revelation of Thomas's early, shadier work did not automatically make my prose any more akin to his. His short fiction can be described as 'hyper-imaginative' in which he confronts reality through fantasy and illusion. My stories could, I suppose, be described as 'hyper-reality,' economical with the facts but at their core, pragmatic and honest. Thomas didn't often use language that could be considered 'bad', if indeed language can be considered 'bad'. It is a 'breast' the Negress bares, 'holding a plate under the black flesh,' in 'Prologue to an Adventure', not a 'tit'. Nevertheless his writing was audacious enough to lead George Reavey of Europa Press to advise Thomas in 1938 that publication of it as it stood 'would lead to imprisonment'. My point is that on that cold afternoon on the Boathouse patio, neither the reader, chairman, nor audience knew those early stories with their ubiquitous themes of sexuality and death existed, that Dylan himself had once been accused of profanity. And if only I had; what a rejoinder I could have thrown at 'Outraged of St Albans'.

So, the question is why didn't I? I knew of the Dylan Thomas caricature, certainly. As I mentioned earlier, my life had been steeped in encounters with *him*. On my first trip to New York in 2001 I'd searched out The White Horse Tavern where he'd apparently drunk those infamous eighteen straight whiskies, and the commemorative plaque on the Chelsea Hotel. I'd seen so many photographs of him, young and moon-faced, and older and bloated with drink, the cigarette butt clinched between fat fingers, I could sketch one from memory. I knew his poetry too, at least 'Do Not Go Gentle into that Good Night' and 'Fern Hill' and 'And Death Shall Have No Dominion', because that's what he was famous for, wasn't it? That's what impressed Robert Zimmerman and convinced him to change his name to Bob Dylan. And that's as it should be. They're percussive and robust, powerhouses of composition. But the hard-drinking legend and the way every committee going has used it as a cash cow for culture-starved post-industrial Wales and the prism of romanticism through which his name seemed to call me, it couldn't allow for the discipline and integrity required in the creation of his intrepid early fiction. It seems ridiculous now to think I once regarded him as fusty and sexless, part of the literary establishment. But I did, and the retired teacher from Hertfordshire thought of him similarly, even if he wouldn't have chosen those words. Perhaps we should beware of how and how much we celebrate and peddle Dylan Thomas, lest we put someone else off.

Dylan and Wilfred Owen

Andrew Lycett

With his track record as a would-be conscientious objector who later spent much of the Second World War turning out well-crafted propaganda for the Crown Film Unit in London, Dylan Thomas is not usually regarded as a war poet.

Nevertheless, although he saw no direct action, Dylan still deserves a place at the top table of those versifiers who have managed to summon up what it means to find oneself in the thick of conflict, if only for his passionate evocations of the pity of war on the home front in poems like 'Deaths and Entrances', 'Among Those Killed in the Dawn Raid was a Man Aged a Hundred' and 'Ceremony after A Fire Raid'.

In these, his mentor, if not his technical model, was Wilfred Owen whom he described in a broadcast for the BBC Eastern Service in July 1946, as 'the greatest poet of the first Great War'. And he added, with the uncomfortable awareness that he was now in the age of the atomic bomb, 'Perhaps, in the future, if there are men, then, still to read – by which I mean, if there are men at all – he may be regarded as one of the great poets of all wars.'

To understand why this singular Welshman had such a strong sense of death and the futility of war, it helps to recall the circumstances of his birth on 27 October 1914, in the middle of the first battle of Ypres. On that day the local battalion of the Welsh Regiment was leaving Swansea to join the British Expeditionary Force in France. One of his earliest memories was his mother coming home from shopping trips and telling his father, 'And do you know who has gone to the front today?' Little Dylan would go to the lobby at the front of the house and look for the person mentioned. 'I could not understand how so many people never returned from there,' he later recalled.

As a result the lyrical rustic who gambolled 'young and easy under the apple boughs ... happy as the grass was green' was always shadowed by an uncompromising realist, insistent that death should have no dominion and urging his father to 'rage against the dying of the light'. His attitude was complicated because his father, D.J. Thomas, had been a non-combatant during the First World War. For reasons which were probably health-related, D.J. had stuck to his job teaching English at Swansea Grammar School. Meanwhile the school itself paid heavily for its involvement in the hostilities: out of around 900 former pupils who served, seventy six were killed. When Dylan went there as a young boy from 1925, he came across an atmosphere of almost exalted reverence for their sacrifice and martial spirit.

D.J. Thomas clearly felt guilty at avoiding the armed forces. According to Daniel Jones, a friend of Dylan's who later became an internationally known composer, the schoolmaster once lost his normal self-control and administered a savage beating to a pupil who had sniggered during a reading from a poet killed in the conflict.

That poet was Wilfred Owen – and his influence (particularly his 'Futility') was clear in one of Dylan Thomas's earliest poems, 'Missing', published in his school magazine in July 1928, when he was thirteen.

> Seek him, thou sun, in the dread wilderness,
> For that he loved thee, seek thou him and bless
> His upturned face with one divine caress.

Dylan continued in this vein in other youthful 'war poems' including 'The Watchers' and 'Armistice Day' (written in 1930), though the Welsh critic James Davies has dismissed these as suburban – closer to Lawrence Binyon than Owen in spirit as 'consoling poems in which the dead are glamorised or inspire fine sentiments in the living'.

But Dylan was expanding his horizons. In a precocious essay on 'Modern Poetry' in his school magazine in December 1929, he argued that the Great War had been the catalyst which 'changed the course of English poetry completely'. Its 'brutality ... failed to warp man's outlook and ideals, and caused some of the bitterest and loveliest poetry in the language to be written'. And he mentions Owen among the 'heroes who built towers of beauty upon the ashes of their lives'. The whole bloody process accelerated moves to poetical modernity which in Thomas's book meant freedom – of form, structure, imagery and idea. It is extraordinary that he had a mature understanding of this while still a teenager.

From the early 1930s he explored these literary devices in his own poetry. And, as he wrote to his unlikely girl friend Pamela Hansford Johnson on Christmas Day 1933, his library at Cwmdonkin Drive, Swansea, was dominated by books of verse, including the *Collected Poems* of Wilfred Owen (probably the 1931 edition by Edmund Blunden).

After moving to London and publishing his first collection *18 Poems* in late 1934, Dylan became an overnight success – a romantic lyrical voice from the provinces who challenged the metropolitan assurance of the dominant Macspaunday group.

With his fiery wit and booming voice, it was not long before he was being sought after as a broadcaster, both for his opinions and for his declamatory skills. On several occasions, starting with *Life and the Modern Poet* in April 1937, he included Owen in his selections of verse for radio, though often packaged as a Welsh poet.

This raises an interesting point about Owen's ancestry. He certainly had Welsh antecedents, though, by the accident of his birth in Oswestry on the Anglo-Welsh borders, he is generally regarded as English. Not that Dylan was particularly interested in such detail. In March 1953, a few months before his death, he explained, with a typical disregard for logic, Owen's inclusion in his latest radio selection: 'Any claim we may make to Wilfred Owen as a Welshman has been repudiated, Anglo-Saxonly and indignantly, by his brother and, I think, his mother. I can defend this choice of poems only by saying that I think they all *sound* well, and that very much of them can by appreciated by a large public at a first hearing. I can't defend my patriotic annexing of [Edward] Thomas & Owen; I like them very much indeed, and that's all.'

Dylan probably had little about the way Owen had himself alluded to his Welshness – for example in the early manuscript for 'Futility' (in the English faculty library at Oxford) which runs:

> Move him into the sun
> Its touch woke him once
> In Wales, whispering of fields unsown.

Towards the end of his short life Owen had written about wanting to write blank-verse plays based on old Welsh themes of the kind known to his ancestors.

Dylan may have sensed that Owen's pararhymes drew inspiration from Welsh verse forms, even if they never imitated the intricate internal rhymes of the *cynghanedd* in the way Manley Hopkins or Thomas himself did.

As was clear from his 1946 talk on Owen for the BBC, Dylan simply regarded the older man as the model poet – uninterested in fame, but 'content to be the unhonoured prophet in death's country'. Owen 'knew, as surely as though the words had been spoken to him aloud, as indeed they had been though they were the words of wounds, the shape of the dead, the colour of blood, he knew he stood alone among men to *plead* for them in their agony, to blast the walls of ignorance, pride, pulpit and state'. Dylan respected Owen's willingness to experiment and his capacity for empathy. 'He writes love-letters home for the illiterate dead. Ignorant, uncaring, hapless as the rest of the bloody troops, he is their arguer shell-shocked into diction, though none may understand.'

On the whole Dylan had little time for any sense of propaganda in verse (one reason for his coolness towards Auden and Spender). But he did not go so far as Yeats who argued that 'Passive suffering is not a theme for poetry' and who therefore refused to include any work by Owen in his *Oxford Book of Modern Verse*, published in 1936.

Dylan was probably telling the truth when he said that he simply liked Owen's sounds. By the 1940s he was at the height of his own powers and prepared to experiment in his own way in a series of poems that centred on the ritualistic nature of death.

The result was a series of mixed messages. On the one hand he could meditate about 'A Refusal to Mourn the Death, by Fire, of a Child in London'. 'After the first death, there is no other.' In such circumstances he suggested that further obsequies seemed not only wrong, but positively obscene.

On the other he could open the organ stops in his grand, swirling 'Ceremony after a Fire Raid'. In this respect he followed Owen whom he had described in his 1946 radio talk as 'the intoning priest over the ceremony ... He is the bell of the church of the broken body.'

Perhaps Thomas's ambivalence about the most appropriate way to commemorate death was an unexpected consequence of his own ability to cross boundaries of time and place and to see what was happening from different perspectives. This is evident in 'Deaths and Entrances', which was his first real war poem (published in 1940 and based on his reaction to the first bombing raids on London). It gave him a title he liked so much that he would use it again for his subsequent book of poems (published in 1946). This collection contained an interesting and popular mixture of searing war poems and intensely lyrical verses such as 'A Poem in October' and 'Fern Hill'.

His original three verse poem 'Deaths and Entrances' drew on John Donne's last sermon 'Death's Duell', which stated that 'Deliverance from that death, the death of the wombe, is a delivery, an entrance over to another death'. The idea was that being born was a form of death. But in the process Dylan was again also paying homage to Wilfred Owen. For the poem played with the perspectives of both the narrator who is the victim of bombing, and the enemy aggressor, a Luftwaffe pilot, in the manner of Owen's 'Strange Meeting'. In this way 'Deaths and Entrances' touched on the horrors experienced by everyone involved in the blitz in much the same way that Owen did with the titanic struggle of the soldiers in the trenches.

One final paradox was that, while Dylan showed no overt sympathies for religion in his daily life, his poetry, particularly when it touched on matters relating to war, could not help taking on a spiritual and even religious dimension. He himself tried to explain this as part of 'the mystery of having been moved by words'. As he added in reply to some questions about his 'craft or sullen art' which were submitted to him by an American research student in 1951, 'The best craftsmanship always leaves holes and gaps in the works of the poem so that something that is not in the poem can creep, crawl, flash, or thunder in. The joy and function of poetry is, and was, the celebration of man, which is also the celebration of God.'

A version of this first appeared in the Newsletter of the Wilfred Owen Association

Curdlers in Their Folly: Welsh Poetry's Retreat from Music in the Years After Dylan

Dai George

Dylan Thomas's premature and wasteful death saddened people the world over, but his abrupt absence presented a particular challenge for Welsh poetry in the English language. To understand the conundrum, one has to step back onto the battlegrounds of the 1960s, the decade immediately after Thomas's death, and one which brought much change to the Anglo-Welsh writing scene with the establishment of the Welsh Writers' Guild in 1964 and *Poetry Wales* the year after that.

A particularly telling and provocative time capsule is available to us in the form of a *Poetry Wales* review by John Idris Jones, written in 1967 to assess a new anthology of Welsh poetry in English, Welsh Voices, edited by Bryn Griffiths. In many places, Jones's article is cranky and rather contradictory about its desires for Welsh poetry, but it is bold and clear on the problem that Dylan Thomas posed for his generation.

> *The new voice which we hear in many of the poems in this anthology is a testimony to the struggles of many writers who are attempting to find a middle way between the highly individual rhetoric of Dylan Thomas and the ordered and rather predictable cadences of R.S. Thomas.*

Such a distinction between our two chief Thomases, Dylan and Ronald Stuart, has become something of a commonplace in discussions of twentieth-century Welsh poetry, but here we have it expressed neatly, at a time when R.S. Thomas's 'massive integrity' – to use Jones's phrase – was still provisional, a work in progress, and Dylan Thomas was scarcely a decade in his grave. Jones's encapsulations of the art of Dylan and R.S. Thomas are uncharitable, to say the least: 'highly individual rhetoric', on one hand, and 'ordered and rather predictable cadences' on the other. These are the twin ogres menacing 1960s Welsh poets in their quest for a viable 'middle way'.

In Jones's view, a handful of the poets in Griffiths's anthology had already succeeded in establishing such a compromise. Taking issue with Griffiths's claim in the introduction that his anthology represented a 'new energy and vigour' among Welsh poets, Jones feels, on the contrary, that the best poetry on offer in *Welsh Voices*

> is exciting and important because, having less *energy and vigour, it is more in the Welsh tradition. It is a tone-of-voice which comes out in Dylan Thomas's later poems, with their superb lyrical quality and tone of mature disillusion: it owes nothing to his earlier energetic rhetorical excesses.*

The poets that Jones selects for particular distinction are Sally Roberts (later Sally Roberts Jones), John Tripp and Herbert Williams, all of whose work attests to 'a combination of aesthetic form, of clarity and maturity, of a determination to tell the truth, of concern with subjects which are actual and real, and of intelligence.'

Whether or not one subscribes to Jones's desiderata, his review gives an indelible flavour of the anxieties at large in Welsh poetry during that decade after Dylan Thomas's death: a time when, in other important ways, the national art was consolidating and growing, with the aid of vital institutional support structures. The overarching anxiety appears to have stemmed from a vague distaste for Thomas's 'rhetorical excesses'; a suppressed antagonism towards his wider fame; and a concomitant obligation – or perceived obligation – to pay lip service to his skill and eminence. (I am not imputing motives here: this chary, ambivalent attitude to Thomas is legible in the two double-edged elegies to him that appear in *Welsh Voices*, Dannie Abse's 'Elegy for Dylan Thomas' and John Tripp's 'Kinder with Him Today'.)

Whatever the precise cocktail of feeling about Thomas among Welsh poets of the '60s, the aesthetic reaction is clear enough to discern. Largely speaking, Welsh poets of that time turned away from Thomas's rich, idiomatic and florid style in favour of a plainer, more democratic language; a language better fit for the communitarian lyric mode that was coming into prominence. Meic Stephens's 'Ponies, Twynyrodyn' is an elegant example of this post-Thomas type of poem. Describing how the ponies come down to Twynyrodyn during a 'bitter spell' of cold weather to disrupt the normal life of the town, it builds to a handsome, analogising finale:

> Now, in this turncoat weather, as
> they lord it through the long terraces,
> toppling bins from wet steps, ribs
> rubbing against the bent railings,
> our smooth blood is disturbed
> by hiraeth for the lost cantrefi...

The intimacy and precision of this description ('ribs/ rubbing against the bent railings') shows how a plainer style needn't sacrifice richness altogether, or a special attention to the sound of words. Indeed, it is off the back of this intelligible, civic language of terraces, bins, wet steps and railings that a grander, more abstract and historical appeal can be made in the final stanza, when the ponies undergo a metamorphosis into 'dark presences of the peasant past', and the 'grim valleys' become 'our common hendre'.

If all poetry to emerge after Dylan Thomas were like 'Ponies, Twynyrodyn', it would be more difficult to voice a reservation. However, Stephens's masterpiece stands at the picturesque summit of plain style, and we run into more problematic questions further down the slopes. Leslie Norris's 'Elegy for Lyn James' derives from a similar community to 'Ponies, Twynyrodyn', but the language it uses to pay tribute to its cast of scrappy small-town boxers has been flattened and lowered to meet that community face-to-face. The opening lines exhibit a bracing disregard for rhetorical excess of any sort: 'I saw your manager fight. He was/ Useful, but his brother had the class.' The first sentence, a refugee from the most basic types of prose, couldn't be any simpler or more expository. The second is more dynamic, engaging the line break to create a brief hesitation, a moment's qualm, before delivering the qualified compliment of 'useful', but still it employs, exclusively, such language as tough, taciturn Valleys men do use: both 'useful' and 'had the class' are received phrases from the 'shabby halls', 'rotting lanes' and 'silent billiard halls' in which the prowess of amateur boxers is routinely discussed.

The sharpness and veracity of Norris's elegy is not at issue, and there is clearly an implied satire in its terse economy of style, which becomes less implied, more didactic in those persistent trochaic adjectives, 'shabby', 'rotting' and 'silent'. But the rolling hills of plain style are many and various, and one has to go to the gentlest foothills in order to diagnose the problem. Another elegy, not from *Welsh Voices* but from Meic Stephens, illustrates my point. Here is the opening stanza from 'An Elegy for Mrs Mordecai':

> Yours was the poorest house in our street:
> the windows were always broken, stopped with rags,
> the porch and passage without a mat. When
> waiting by the door for my butties, your strapping boys,
> I had to hold my breath against the stench.

Honest, vivid, and effective description, yes – but also a little baggy and lacking shape, a little bit documentary. Worse, the shared, colloquial language of the poem, which initially seeks to honour Mrs Mordecai in her poverty, comes gradually to collude with the slanders of its community, as the speaker blithely tells her, 'You/ were famous in the Rhydyfelen pubs as Fag Ash Lil,// a painted bag whose charms were blown.' Never mind, though, because Mrs Mordecai's great virtue was to command in her offspring 'a loyalty/ (some call it love) that was by no means common.' Whenever there was a problem on her doorstep, her children 'would be there, taking [her] side',

> the girls in their high heels, blonde as
> Monroe and brazen too, the brothers all made good by now
> not looking for trouble but nonetheless quick
> to flash their knives or fivers for their mother's sake.

Condescension is one pitfall of a plain, democratic style, but not the only one. Aside from this ethical danger, there is an aesthetic loss, which Jones in his review of *Welsh Voices* sums up well, if in an old-fashioned way. Surveying the 'similarity of the subjects and methods' in the anthology, he laments:

> *If only there was a funny poem ... a very short, precise poem... poems which showed a real awareness of new tendencies in American verse ... this American sense of the immediate, of the sensory present, would be an antidote to our Welsh tendency to be 'heavy,' explicit and didactic. When we turn away from music, which is the Welshness in us, we tend to fall too easily into the prosaic.*

I imagine most people today would turn away from any notion that music 'is the Welshness in us', whatever that might mean. But that word 'music', which until now I have avoided, may yet explain the strange fault line that lies between the poetry of Thomas's lifetime and the poetry that emerged for a decade or two in his wake. Did Welsh poets of the late-1950s and '60s abjure music, whether consciously or otherwise? It is easy enough to establish that they wrote differently from Thomas, but much harder to claim that 'music', or the lack of music, is the difference. 'Music', as it stands in relation to poetry, is a slippery term that Jones makes no attempt in his article to define. As 'Ponies, Twynyrodyn' demonstrates, poetry can sound good – can roll easily off the tongue – without being overtly rhythmic, assonant or technical. Whatever definition of poetic music might be available to us, surely we would want it to encompass that poem's quiet, suggestive and honed language. Yet, to do justice to the range of what we hear in different types of poetry, there must be varying degrees of music, with the subtle, undulating language of 'Ponies, Twynyrodyn' sitting towards one end of a spectrum, while the early work of Dylan Thomas occupies the other extremity.

So what on earth do we mean when we call a poem 'musical'? Hopefully we can dispense with the tempting, facile definition that musical poetry 'sounds good'. Often it will, but plenty of unmusical prose can have a ring to it, and some of the most musical poetry may not sound good, at least not in any conventional sense, just as 'sounds good' might not be the most appropriate thing to say about a Shostakovich symphony. Musical poetry can be rebarbative, dissonant, cloying, demanding, or otherwise excessive. Dylan Thomas – who was almost always musical – could be all of those things, sometimes several at once, and usually at least one of those adjectives is lurking behind even his most impressive moments. Nevertheless, we undervalue and mistake Thomas's art if we see him as being engaged essentially in a noble struggle against his most musical tendencies ('his earlier energetic rhetorical excesses'), expunging them over the course of his career in a quest towards that 'superb lyrical quality and tone of mature disillusion' in the later poems. On the contrary, Dylan Thomas's command of music was present to an astonishing degree in his first collection, *18 Poems*, published when he was only twenty. The mistake lies in any assumption that music at that stage had the command of Thomas, rather than the other way around.

18 Poems is a highly controlled performance. Across its pages I can discern at least three governing principles in its composition, which may also serve as some preliminary definitions of 'musical poetry', if we are that way inclined. First, its management of syntax resists the clarity of 'good' prose, often by using long, circuitous subordinate clauses to begin poems. For me, this is the most important thing in distinguishing musical from unmusical or not-so-musical poetry; all other definitions might be said to derive from it. Prose should be a very different sort of cloth from poetry, yet it's woven from the same basic fibre of the sentence. A prose sentence – particularly the first sentence in any prose paragraph, and *particularly* the first sentence in an article, essay or chapter – will often seek to establish its subject matter by firmly rooting us in a stable, active grammatical subject. This is one reason why some of the poems I have looked at in this essay bear a curious, double-take resemblance to prose: their opening sentences start unambiguously with the subject of the sentence, and sometimes it's a very simple sentence indeed.

I saw your manager fight.

Yours was the poorest house on our street...

Even the glorious opening sentence of 'Ponies, Twynyrodyn' employs the clear, subject-setting tactic of prose:

Winter, the old drover, has brought
these beasts from the high moor's hafod
to bide the bitter spell among us,
here, in the valley streets.

In this case, however, the rhythm of the prose sentence receives a gentle disruption almost immediately, with the insertion of a metaphorical subordinate clause ('the old drover') between the subject of the sentence and its main verb. Indeed, these four lines spool out in a patient, lilting, cumulative way, quite different from the swift fixity of the two opening sentences from the elegies to Lyn James and Mrs Mordecai. It is a large part of why 'Ponies, Twynyrodyn' reaches for a condition nearer to music than prose.

However, it is still a good deal nearer to prose than this one-sentence opening stanza from *18 Poems*.

Especially when the October wind
With frosty fingers punishes my hair,
Caught by the crabbing sun I walk on fire
And cast a shadow crab upon the land,
By the sea's side, hearing the noise of birds,
Hearing the raven cough in winter sticks,
My busy heart who shudders as she talks
Sheds the syllabic blood and drains her words.

There is more than one way to read this. You could say that the independent clause begins in the third line ('I walk on fire/ And cast a shadow crab upon the land'), but I tend to read that as being nested in a second subordinate clause, so that 'Caught by the crabbing sun' follows from 'when' in the first line. The same is then true for several other sub-clauses ('By the sea's side' and the two consecutive 'hearing' clauses): they all rely upon the reader's memory of 'when' in the first line, to deliver the emphatic independent clause of the final two lines, where a line break is employed to insist upon the active clarity of the main verb ('Sheds'). However you read it, though, there can be little doubt that the poem creates a radically less stable experience for the reader than any of the post-Thomas poems we have looked at, and that instability is part of the quality of music. Unsure of when to latch onto the stanza and treat it as she might an ordinary prose sentence, the reader has to submit instead to the sound of the words, entertaining each fragmentary clause in turn, as a sonic event first and a possible resolution second, before finally meeting with a semblance of clarity at the last moment. She has to listen to the cadence of the sentence very carefully to determine when it resolves, and rely upon instinct as much as judgement to hear that.

The second pronounced musical quality in *18 Poems* is its sense of patterning. Like complex sentences, patterns estrange poetry from straightforward prose meaning, though in a crucially different way. Where Thomas's complex sentences seem almost intentionally to wrong-foot readers, his patterns affirm our intelligence and set up fair expectations that are more often than not met. Even when the reader doesn't feel that she quite understands what Thomas is going on about, she can rely upon metrical feet and the predictable return of phrases to supply different kinds of salience. This is by definition a musical tactic, since it asks us to check our conscious understanding of language and to glean meaning equally, if not primarily, from how it sounds and how it recurs.

'I See the Boys of Summer' provides the most glittering, and some might say obsessive, example of pattern-making in the poetry of any era. Part 1 of the poem establishes an intense, interweaving set of correspondences between its four six-line stanzas. The rhyme scheme of each stanza (AABCBC) is by far the least remarkable thing about it, though the half and near rhymes are strikingly partial for their time –

the sort of sound correspondence that merrily yokes together 'folly' and 'honey', hearing in both words a falling, lavish music far more important than the full rhyme between 'folly' and, say, 'holly'. Indeed, this fall gives rise to the first, exciting pattern of the poem, which the reader hears more immediately than any rhyme.

> I see the boys of summer in their ruin
> Lay the gold tidings barren...

All four stanzas of part I open with the same metrical rhythm: a handsome, complete, though feminine line of iambic pentameter, followed by an emaciated seven-syllable line, which starts on the stress of a verb before falling away to another feminine ending.

> These boys of light are curdlers in their folly,
> Sour the boiling honey...
>
> I see the summer children in their mothers
> Split up the brawned womb's weathers...
>
> I see that from these boys shall men of nothing
> Stature by seedy shifting...

This is the music of orgasmic dissipation, of promising young boys turning into 'men of nothing'. The verb at the start of each second line could represent a moment of ejaculation, which soon gives way to the languorous, spent energy of 'boiling honey', 'womb's weathers' and 'seedy shifting'.

We can be reasonably quick in saying that the work of Norris, Stephens and several other poets in *Welsh Voices* creates nothing like such an innovative or direct compact between the sound of the poem and its meaning. Their poems are largely written in unrhymed lines that hover around the four- or five-beat mark, with a sharp eye for the line break but little attempt at patterning beyond the occasional regularity of stanza-length (for instance, 'Elegy for Lyn James', which comes as three stanzas of seven lines). The effect is akin to that of reading an essay, where the form will stretch endlessly to accommodate the thing that needs to be said. In a Thomas poem, on the other hand, one is aware of constraint as well as of liberty and amplitude; the language is made to bend to form in a way quite alien to the democratic poetries of the '60s. A last aspect of poetic music I would like to comment on relates to these systems of patterning and recursion in *18 Poems*. Many modern critics might look askance at the grand symbolic language at play in Dylan Thomas's first collection, seeing a juvenile lack of variety or specificity in its lexicon of hearts, tombs, shrouds, earth, sky, sun and – most consistently, and for some ludicrously – worms. I don't wish to argue with those who find this circling repetition of nouns exasperating; it tries my patience too, especially when gorged upon in one extended sitting. But, again, I suspect that we give Thomas too little credit if we read these early poems as being helplessly in thrall to symbolism, and not active participants in the creation of a new, robust symbolic language.

This question of symbolism is at root a musical question because, when poetry retreats from material particularity to archetype, it fosters a new relationship between the reader and the meanings and sounds of words. When we hear the word 'womb' or 'worm' recur so often as we do in *18 Poems*, we quickly cease to imagine any particular womb or worm; the meanings and images are available to us if we care to remember them, but the primary response shifts to being a sonic one. We hear them as repeated motifs, in a similar way to how themes in a symphony return and stimulate an ear trained to listen for them. But that stimulation, that sense of recognition, can turn into an irritant as well as a tonic, and flowery, prodigious early Dylan Thomas certainly has ample capacity to irritate. There is but one main theme in *18 Poems*, though it is as various, universal and complex a subject as anyone could hope to find: a young man's conviction that life and death are driven by the same force; that beauty and mortality are locked in a waltz; that, 'The signal grass that tells me all I know/ Breaks with the wormy winter through the eye.' Unfortunately for Dylan Thomas's reputation, it is also a theme that will strike many experienced poetry readers as hackneyed and immature.

By the time that *Welsh Voices* had been published in 1967, Welsh poetry had largely renounced such majestic, totalizing themes in favour of the social lyric mode. (There are, as ever, exceptions, not least in Glyn Jones, whose poetry retained throughout the '60s and beyond a mysterious, delicate music informed by Dylan Thomas, only with a lighter touch.) The social lyric has an infinity of themes, from boxers, to ponies, to meditations on exile and separation from one's hometown. Insofar as music is an apt analogy at all for the work of Leslie Norris and Meic Stephens, and beyond them Dannie Abse, John Tripp, Gillian Clarke, Tony Conran, Peter Gruffydd, Harri Webb and Raymond Garlick, their music is that of a prelude, a miniature, or an etude, in direct contrast to the symphonic aggregations of *18 Poems*. Of course, many people prefer Philip Glass to Richard Wagner, and a good handful of the post-Thomas poets I have listed went on to create work of lasting value and impressive range, to say nothing of popularity. However, it seems harder than ever to deny that something important was lost in Welsh poetry's transition from the dark, Thomas-dominated days of the late-1950s to the dynamic and thriving writing culture that arose with the advent of *Poetry Wales*.

'Curdlers in their folly' is a harsh phrase to brand on anyone's forehead, whether they are Thomas's wanton boys of summer, or else good poets who did much to create the cultural weather that Welsh writers nowadays take for granted. Nonetheless, there is a nuance in that neologism, 'curdler', that is too tempting to ignore. Too often in that decade Welsh poetry did curdle, becoming bogged down in particular themes and modes of civic address at the expense of a more primary concern with music and sound. The folly of this change will vary with the eye of each beholder, but I think Dannie Abse coined an interesting and prescient phrase in his 'Elegy for Dylan Thomas', when he spoke of the need for poets to travel, in Thomas's footsteps, 'far from the blind country of prose'.

Portrait in Wisteria: an Ekphrastic Meditation on Dylan Thomas

Sarah Gridley

Photographer Rosalie Thorne ('Rollie') McKenna met Dylan Thomas through their mutual friend, John Malcolm Brinnin, in 1952. This was on Thomas's second trip to America. His fourth and final trip would end in his death less than a year later. In his introduction to McKenna's *Portrait of Dylan: A Photographer's Memoir*, Brinnin wrote, 'So began a friendship between them that made possible a photographic record of Dylan's last years unique in its opportunities and unmatched in its range and variety.'[1] Of the many photographs McKenna took of Thomas, she chose one in particular to appear on the jacket cover of the book (as a black and white insert overlying a colour photograph of the estuary flats at Laugharne), and again, in full length, on the title page. McKenna remembered the shoot from which this photo emerged:

> *To go back to my first meeting with Dylan and Caitlin is to go back to a cold January evening in 1952, at my home in Millbrook, New York ... Next morning, the fields a dazzling white, the sky blue and clear, the sun bright and the wind sharp, Dylan, John and I started outside for a short walk and picture-taking ... Dylan spotted a large bare wisteria vine and immediately entwined himself in it, laughing, smiling, smirking, then sinking as if crucified... I used up several rolls of film on Dylan by the wisteria...*[2]

The jacket cover/title page photograph is one of a number of photographs in this wisteria series. What made McKenna select this one for the jacket cover and title page? What made it *the* portrait of *Portraits*?

In 'Understanding a Photograph,' John Berger reminds us that a photograph is as much a gesture toward an absented continuum as it is a relic of a given moment. In Berger's words: 'What it shows invokes what is not shown.'³ A photographer appraises a photograph by way of a particular calculus: 'The degree to which I believe this is worth looking at can be judged by all that I am willingly not showing because it is contained within it.'⁴ To clarify this, Berger supplies concrete examples: 'The immediate relation between what is present and what is absent is particular to each photograph,' he writes, 'it may be that of ice to sun, of grief to a tragedy, of a smile to a pleasure, of a body to love...'⁵ A viewer feels, in the visible features of a photograph, some specimen of a speaking, absent whole. What distinguishes a memorable photograph from a commonplace one is how intensely it calls up these poles of presence and absence. What can be seen in a photograph is indebted to what cannot be seen, which is to say, a field of experience inclusive of, but greater than, the frame.

The photograph McKenna chose for the jacket cover/title page shows Thomas from his shins up, and includes in its frame some of the wisteria's supporting structure, McKenna's white clapboard house. Wisteria is a woody vine and so retains a substantial – one might say sculptural – presence in winter. The vine climbs by twisting either clockwise or counterclockwise around an available support. The bodyline Thomas arrived at in response to the whorls of wisteria reminds me of Donatello's David. Though it is his right knee that is bent, as opposed to David's left, the effect on the hips is the same: a curve connoting a slight weight shift. Because Thomas is wearing heavy tweed trousers and a wool sweater, the line loses some of its sinuosity to bulkiness, but the posture is similarly languid. With elbows bent, Thomas grips the wisteria, though the path of two vines crossing at his chest suggests he is already supported – in effect caged or girdled – by the vine.

McKenna remembered the winter morning as one of clear blue skies, sharp wind, and bright sunlight. The length of Thomas's right side is reproduced in shadow on the clapboard, intermingled with wisteria shadows. Because the frame only includes Thomas's body from the shins up, one cannot see his feet. From the knee downward, the checks of his tweed trousers go black in shadow. His lower legs and feet are occluded, as is the trunk of wisteria. As though in diagonal sympathy with the vine that makes up one half of the 'X' across his chest, Thomas's head leans to his right. His face is framed by a dark shirt and darker sweater. His only visible ear (the left one), is bathed in light. While the greater part of this photograph is taken up by Thomas's entwinement, other 'background' elements are worth noting. The horizontal lines of clapboard are crossed by the vertical line of what looks to be either a support beam or downspout (a clue to McKenna's impression that Thomas was 'sinking as if crucified'). Thomas's spine almost aligns with its verticality, but doesn't quite, due to the bent knee posture I've described. Between clapboard lines, on line with Thomas's groin, there is a small-sized sill cock, an outdoor water spigot. Beneath this, between the next lower down pair of clapboard lines, a telephone line, painted white to match the house, runs horizontally before disappearing into Thomas's right-side shadow.

These are the visible elements of the title page photograph, as best as I can describe them, and omitting a description of Thomas's facial expression, which I will return to after a detour, during which I ask a reader to hold this image of the poet's vegetal entwinement in mind. Before exploring, à la Berger, the absent elements this photograph conjures for me, I'd like to discuss a few ideas that have been important to my thinking about Dylan Thomas, and in turn, to my own work as a poet.

Dylan Thomas: a Collection of Critical Essays came out in 1966. Edited by C.B. Cox, it presents a range of perspectives on Dylan Thomas, some positive, some not. It includes essays by notable Thomas scholars – John Ackerman, Ralph Maud, and John Wain – and by critics moved (or itching) to evaluate his legacy in the wake of his death – John Bayley, William Empson, and Karl Shapiro. In 'The Welsh Background,' John Ackerman set out to uncover the Welsh roots of Thomas's poetry, to go beyond – or perhaps beneath – the abundant Freudian readings of the poems. While he acknowledged the impact of Freudian psychology on the young Thomas, Ackerman said the arc of Thomas's poetry moved from 'the clinical towards a religious purpose'.[6] For Ackerman, this religious purpose coincided with the poet's deepened sense of belonging to a Welsh cultural tradition. He reprinted Thomas's note to the *Collected Poems* as a starting point for this exploration:

> *I read somewhere of a shepherd, who, when asked why he made, from within fairy rings, ritual observances to the moon to protect his flocks, replied: 'I'd be a damned fool if I didn't!' These poems, with all their crudities, doubts, and confusions, are written for the love of Man and in praise of God, and I'd be a damn' fool if they weren't.*

Ackerman identified 'a bardic ring' in this statement: 'Thomas is claiming a high function for the poet, though as usual there is a 'dog among the fairies mocking wisdom...'[7] Ackerman heard 'defensive irony' in this presentation, a 'mocking wisdom'; I hear something else. A pragmatic approach to religion, which William James laid out for us in *The Varieties of Religious Experience*, takes both a loose and a rigorous approach to divinity: 'the word 'divine' ... shall mean for us only such a primal reality as the individual feels impelled to respond to solemnly and gravely, and neither by a curse nor a jest'.[8] Pragmatism is what keeps us from the easy, slippery slopes of irony. For Ackerman, fairies are what colour the statement with irony; one could only be jesting re: fairy rings. But a 1934 letter to Trevor Hughes suggests the youthful Thomas viewed fairies quite *un*-ironically: 'The new year has brought back to mind the sense of magic that was lost – irretrievably, I thought – so long ago. I am conscious, if not of the probability of the impossible, at least of its possibility, and the paradox has clothed itself like a fairy ... A fairy is not supernatural; she is the most natural thing in the world.'[9] James insisted on the solemnity of the religious experience, however idiosyncratic an experience of the divine it might be. The shepherd was for Thomas a model religious practitioner because he directed his attention to the supernatural pragmatically, concentrically (as opposed to eccentrically), with the ritual observance of fairy rings.

Form or incorporation might be another way to think about this. In Thomas's letter, impossible possibility – that paradox – is perceptible to the poet because it has taken on the *clothing* of a fairy, which is to say an ethereal-corporeal appearance. In another letter, Thomas defended his reliance on the corporeal as a method of contacting the astral bodies of stars. Speaking of his poems, he wrote:

> *They are, I admit, unpretty things, with their imagery almost totally anatomical. But I defend the diction, the perhaps wearisome succession of blood and bones, the neverending similes of the streams in the veins and the lights in the eyes, by saying that, for the time at least, I realize that it is impossible for me to raise myself to the altitude of the stars, and that I am forced, therefore, to bring down the stars to my own level and to incorporate them in my own physical universe.*[10]

Poems have their own anatomies, their own outward contours and inward regulations. Ackerman reminds us that Thomas was painstakingly interested in – one could say devoted to – the shaping work of poetry, the possibility that a poem might body forth something beyond the materials of the poem. Perhaps this grounding and reaching dynamic is where the pragmatic and the bardic cross through each other:

> *... it must be remembered that the discipline of Welsh bardic poetry is among the strictest in any known literature. It was written in elaborate metres, and continues to be to the present day. Herein is the paradox of the bardic tradition. The exuberance of the bardic personality, the liking for ceremony and elaborate ritual, co-exist with a most crafstmanlike devotion to composition.*[11]

After pointing thus to the performative paradox of the bardic tradition – extravagant and painstaking – Ackerman discussed its paradoxical conception of existence. He cited a passage from the *Mabinogion* that Gwyn Williams, a scholar of early Welsh poetics, pointed to in *The Burning Tree*: 'And they saw a tall tree by the side of the river, one half of which was in flames from the root to the top, and the other half was green and in full leaf.'[12] Williams, as Ackerman relayed, saw the Celtic tree as a 'hitherto unapprehended relation of things, an integration of spring and autumn...' [13]We can hear versions (or visions) of this Celtic tree – its entwinement of contraries – in two Thomas letters. In the aforementioned letter containing fairies, he wrote: 'It is my aim as an artist ... to bring those wonders into myself, to prove beyond doubt to myself that the flesh that covers me is the flesh that covers the sun, that the blood in my lungs is the blood that goes up and down in a tree. It is the simplicity of religion.'[14] In a letter to Charles Fisher a year later, Thomas wrote: 'You asked me to tell you about my theory of poetry. Really I haven't got one ... I like 'redeeming the contraries' with secretive images ... Poetry ... should be as orgiastic and organic as copulation, dividing and unifying, personal but not private, propagating the individual in the mass and the mass in the individual.'[15] It is easy to understand copulation in its sexual sense here (Thomas was after all twenty one at the time of this letter), but we can also take its meaning – to fasten together – in another sense, a logical and grammatical one. A copula, in this context, is a connecting word, a form of the verb *to be* connecting a subject and a complement. In America, we call these 'linking verbs.' Thomas's vision of copulation opens in two directions at once: sexual and linguistic.

In his superb study, *Poets of Reality*, J. Hillis Miller explained that for Thomas, 'consciousness has no separate existence, but exists in interpenetration with all things'.[16] Given this dynamic interpenetration of mind, body, and world, things are verbal rather than substantial: 'in such a universe things are what they do.'[17] Linking Miller's reading with Thomas's letter, we might say that things are *copulative*, though in the case of linking verbs, or copulae, *doing* is replaced by *being*, and specifically, *being-in-relation-to*. Thomas was extraordinarily fond of the verbal adjective, as Miller pointed out. He would write 'a robin-breasted tree' where another poet might write 'a tree full of robins.' Miller unpacked this idiom: 'The tree and its robins do not exist in isolation from one another, but share each other's life. The robins are attributes of the tree. The tree is robin breasted.'[18] *The tree is robin breasted.* Copula, it turns out, is the grammatical blueprint for metaphor, what Owen Barfield in *Poetic Diction* called 'the most conspicuous point of contact between meaning and poetry'.[19]

Some consider metaphor a matter of invention. Others see it as a matter of discovery. I think you can tell a lot about a person by which understanding he or she has of metaphor, the former, or the latter. In the latter metaphor is new for the mind, not for the world. As Barfield explained, 'Men do not *invent* those mysterious relations between separate and external objects ... These relations exist independently...'[20] In a baffling line of argument, Karl Shapiro, appearing in the same Cox anthology as Ackerman, painted Dylan Thomas as a metaphor-maker manqué: 'Unlike Hopkins, he has no vision of nature and cannot break open the forms of nature; he cannot break open words. He focuses madly on the object, but it will not yield. He calls a weathercock a bow-and-arrow bird. Metaphor won't come and he resorts to riddle, the opposite of metaphor.'[21] Leaving aside the thorny issue of whether riddle does in fact work in direct opposition to metaphor, one has to wonder what manner of blinders and earplugs and general grumpiness was at work in Shapiro's reading of Thomas (Thomas, our poet of 'vowelled beeches' and 'each red particle'). The figure of a 'bow-and-arrow bird' is not a failed attempt to 'break open the forms of nature'; it is a site of nature-being-fastened-with-human-habitation. It is a site of bird totem, wind, and the ancient human desire to 'know which way the wind blows' – meteorically and metaphysically. It is not a riddle whose answer is weathercock. It is, like robin-breasted tree, a way of seeing and saying relation.

Poet James Dickey saw metaphor as the footwork of a mind that could never apprehend itself in full. Metaphor is adventurous because it works by bits and pieces, which is to say, temporally: 'The relation of poetry – and metaphor – to the self ... is a matter of moments, and of the conjunctions that may be born of the moment, and illuminate the moment, and then come to stand for one of the ways in which the moment may strike to the heart of time itself.'[22] To strike to the heart of time is to annul past, present, and future. Dickey called this space *materia mater*. While this is the source from which all associations issue, it is a source associable with no thing we can name or know. It is the un-compassable, incomparable source of all *being-in-relation-to*.

Holding open the impossible possibility that a moment might strike to 'the heart of time itself,' I would like to return to John Berger, who argued that the choice a photographer makes in her art is primarily temporal, not compositional, as it is for a painter: 'I have said that a photograph bears witness to a human choice being exercised. This choice is not between photographing x and y: but between photographing at x moment or at y moment.'[23] Photography finds its 'proper' meaning (by which I understand Berger to mean its very own, its unique meaning) 'between the poles of presence and absence'.[24] For Berger, time, more so than space, is *the* defining mediator, the preeminent arbiter of 'in' and 'beyond' the frame.

Before returning to an exploration of what is absent in McKenna's portrait of Thomas entwined with wisteria, I'd like to spend a moment considering what *might* have been absented from this photograph in a photoshopped world. I mentioned, among the contents of the photograph, a sill cock, or little water spigot, on level with Thomas's groin. Against the pathos of this photograph, for Thomas's facial expression, which I held off describing, is uncannily solemn, this little 'cock' introduces some comic naughtiness and/or Freudian intrigue for those likely to think along such lines. Sometimes a sill cock is just a sill cock, undoubtedly, but its presence in *this* photograph invites the possibility of pathos plummeting to bathos. Today, a digital photographer could photo shop 'out' the sill cock, and possibly the distracting phone line, too. Horizontal clapboard would then be the dignified backdrop to a 'crucified' Thomas. I for one am grateful McKenna didn't have this option. To crop out the sill cock would have been an option, only it would have meant cropping out shadows Thomas cast on the clapboard.

Considering what *might have been absent* from this photo helps me think through the following Berger statement: 'The immediate relation between what is present and what is absent is particular to each photograph ... it may be that of ice to sun, of grief to tragedy, of a smile to pleasure, of a body to love...'[25] At first, I understood Berger to be describing a *causal* relationship between an outside-the-frame stimulus and an inside-the-frame response. Then I realised the relation is better described as synecdochical/metonymic: 'A photograph is effective when the chosen moment it records contains a quantum of truth which is generally applicable ... All this may seem close to the old principle of art transforming the particular into the universal. But photography does not deal in constructs. There is no transforming in photography. There is only decision, only focus.'[26] A causal relation would mean this thing is evident *because* of that absent thing. Berger's idea is that a thing inside the frame is meaningful by way of metaphor, or (grammatically speaking) copulation (this fastening to that). If the sill cock in question can be read as a visible part in relation to an absent whole, the absent whole might be Dylan Thomas's singularly and cosmically marvelous sense of humour. In his introduction to *Portrait of Dylan*, John Malcolm Brinnin wrote, 'The pensive and the raucous Dylan are here, and so are the searching eyes of a man of genius and the lurking mischief of a little boy trying to be bad'.[27] There is an echo here of the 'truant' boys that populate Thomas's beautiful poem, 'The Hunchback in the Park,' a poem that, like the photograph, imagines the entwinement of the human and the vegetal ('A woman figure without fault/ Straight as a young elm'). Like many Thomas poems, this is a poem of patterned contraries: the human and the animal ('old dog sleeper'); the jurisdictional and the fluid ('From the opening of the garden lock/ That lets the trees and water enter'); the gracefully formed (swans) and the deformed (hunchback). But nowhere, with the notable exception of 'Fern Hill,' do the contrary states of boyhood and manhood cross so painfully and strike so beautifully at the heart of time.

In McKenna's portrait of Thomas, synecdoche is traveling two ways: the boy part (the little sill cock) is standing in for the whole host of sexual predicaments Thomas attempted to work through as a grownup poet (what Ackerman calls the 'clinical' part of his development); conversely, the man of the portrait stands in for the multiple parts of his 'once below a time' childhood. Present in the photograph by way of absence is the 'heart of time' vision we feel in lines like 'boys innocent as strawberries' and 'Time held me green and dying/ Though I sang in my chains like the sea.' In such lines the separately imagined poles of presence and absence – of time occupied and time lost – cross improbably, inimitably, and indelibly. Thomas could strike so musically at the heart of time because he struck so mercilessly. In the wisteria series photograph McKenna chose for the title page of *Portrait of Dylan*, this X is both a powerfully speaking absence, and a visibly present detail (the crossing vines). I think what distinguished this photograph from others in the series is that playacting was overtaken by veritable ensorcellment. The poles of presence and absence Berger describes cross weirdly and unforgettably, catching in Thomas's vegetal imprisonment a profound mood of transportment.

I have kept a copy of this portrait of Dylan Thomas in my wallet, a postcard version of it, for nearly twenty-five years. It lives besides another photograph that is precious to me, a picture of me and my brother as small children feeding ducks in the early 1970s. Keeping this Thomas photograph close to me is my own version of a fairy ring, a ritual observance. Wallace Stevens wrote in a letter 'People ought to like poetry the way a child likes snow & they would if poets wrote it'.[28] Thomas, one of our great poets of snow and childhood – 'I can never remember whether it snowed for six days and six nights when I was twelve or whether it snowed for twelve days and twelve nights when I was six' – calls us to be poetic religiously and religious poetically, which I think means holding fast to the intertwined wonders we experienced through childhood consciousness – robin breasted trees among them. Some find this call embarrassing. Michael Robbins, a fellow American poet, writes of Dylan Thomas, 'Perhaps I'd love him more if I hadn't loved him so much, so early'. Robbins' essay, 'The Child That Sucketh Long,' is an exorcism of influence: 'So get you gone, Dylan Thomas, though with blessings on your head.'[29] Dylan Thomas was also an early crush for me. Unlike Robbins, I've never felt the need to disavow him. This essay, with all its crudities, doubts, and confusions, was written for the love of Dylan Thomas and in praise of him, and I'd be a damn fool if it weren't.

1 John Malcolm Brinnin, Introduction to *Portrait of Dylan: a Photographer's Memoir*, by Rollie McKenna (Stemmer House Publishers, Inc., 1982), 10.

2 Ibid., 56.

3 John Berger, 'Understanding a Photograph,' in *Selected Essays*, edited by Geoff Dyer (Vintage, 2003), Kindle edition.

4/5 Ibid.

6 John Ackerman, 'The Welsh Background,' in *Dylan Thomas: a Collection of Critical Essays*, ed. C.B. Cox (Prentice-Hall, Inc., 1966), 26.

7 Ibid., 28.

8 William James, *The Varieties of Religious Experience*, edited by Martin E. Marty (Viking Penguin, Inc., 1982), 38.

9 Dylan Thomas, *The Collected Letters of Dylan Thomas*, edited by Paul Ferris (J.M. Dent & Sons, Ltd., 1985), 91.

10 Ibid., 90.

11 Ackerman, in 'The Welsh Background,' in *Dylan Thomas: a Collection of Critical Essays*, ed. C.B. Cox, 29.

12/13 Ibid.

14 Dylan Thomas, in *The Collected Letters*, edited by Paul Ferris, 89-90.

15 Ibid.,181-182.

16 J. Hillis Miller, *Poets of Reality* (The Belknap Press of Harvard University Press, 1965), 198.

17/18 Ibid., 197-198.

19 Owen Barfield, *Poetic Diction: A Study in Meaning* (Wesleyan University Press, 1973), 63.

20 Ibid., 86. Prior to this statement, Barfield quotes Bacon's *Advancement of Learning*: 'Neither are these only similitudes, as men of narrow observation may conceive them to be, but the same foot-steps of nature, treading or printing upon several subjects or matters.'

21 Karl Shapiro, 'Dylan Thomas' in *Dylan Thomas: a Collection of Critical Essays*, edited by C.B. Cox (Prentice-Hall, Inc., 1966), 177.

22 James Dickey, 'Metaphor as Pure Adventure' (lecture, the Library of Congress, Washington, DC, 1968).

23 John Berger, 'Understanding a Photograph,' in *Selected Essays*, edited by Geogg Dyer. Kindle edition.

24/25/26 Ibid.

27 John Malcolm Brinnin, Introduction to *Portait of Dylan: a Photographer's Memoir*, by Rollie McKenna, 10.

28 Wallace Stevens, *Letters of Wallace Stevens*, edited Holly Stevens (University of California Press, 1996), 349.

29 Michael Robbins, 'The Child That Sucketh Long,' Poetry Foundation, originally published January 2, 2013, www.poetryfoundation.org/poetrymagazine/article/245156.

No Sullen Art

Sarah King

On 23 May, 1953, Dylan Thomas wrote in a letter to his wife: 'I have finished that infernally, eternally, unfinished play'. He was talking about *Under Milk Wood*, the radio play that had its embryonic beginnings when Thomas was only seventeen, and which he would visit, revisit, despair and obsess over until, twenty-two years later, the last pages were finally dragged out of him after being locked in a room by his literary agent. Six months after writing the letter he fell into an alcohol induced coma and never woke up.

Peter Blake was then still a young student at the Royal College of Art and heard *Under Milk Wood* when it was first read on the radio in 1954. Blake went on to become one of England's premier Pop artists, creating the cover for The Beatles' *Sgt Pepper's Lonely Hearts Club Band* while developing a unique, fascinating and iconic mixed-media and collage style. *Under Milk Wood* stayed with him, and when he rediscovered it twenty-five year later he was, as he says, 'trapped'. Illustrating the play became on ongoing project he would visit, off and on, for the next 30 years. As he puts it: 'It's like throwing a stone into water. The ripples have just got bigger and bigger, and wider and wider.'

I visited the upstairs gallery at National Museum Cardiff several times between November 2013 and March 2014 to see the results of Blake's obsession, to try to make sense of the spider's web of imagery, and see Dylan Thomas's words through someone else's eyes.

Under Milk Wood starts in the dark. The listener floats, like a spectre through the night, listening to the people of Llareggub's dreams and desires. When day breaks we hear them wake, work, gossip, sing, complain, love, hate and desire their way through a day in the little fishing town.

The illustrations are literal depictions of the story. When Thomas writes about farmer Utah Watkins counting wife-faced sheep in his dreams, Blake paints a sheep's body with a woman's face and human, knitting hands and a docile smile. When Thomas writes about the 'titbits and topsyturvies' bobbing in the sea, Blake creates a collage of buttons, animal skulls, seashells and glass bottles floating on grey, dull waves. And when Thomas tells us about the babies and old men washed and put in their broken prams, Blake shows the viewer a comical image of grumpy old, bearded faces cut and pasted to peek out of Victorian prams. On the blank canvas given to him by the radio play, Blake shows the viewer everything he hears. Blake, like Thomas, sees the absurdity in people. His illustrations are not only tender and evocative, they are also funny and at times grotesque. Little snippets of text are written underneath the images in Blake's small, intricate handwriting. A constant reminder of the source and inspiration.

Back at the museum.

'Look... that's a really big one!' I hear a child's voice behind me. Without looking around, I know what has captured the child's attention. I smile.

Polly Garter sings about her many lovers, and Peter Blake draws the naked torsos of a woman and four men. One man lounging on a chair, his ridiculously over sized penis flopping onto his leg. The child's mam is flustered and quickly leads her away. I meet my friend. We look at a watercolour of the widow Ogmore-Pritchard. Sleeping and dreaming of her two dead husbands.

'That's not how I see Mrs Ogmore-Pritchard,' she says. We look for a while at the illustration, at the ghosts of the husbands resting on either side of her, on clean white pillows.

Mrs Ogmore-Pritchard is so uptight and obsessed with cleanliness she makes the sun wipe its shoes before she lets it in, but Blake pictures her soft, hair down and with a blank expression on her sleeping face. My friend, poignantly, says: 'He must see something I don't.' In a play for words the audience makes their own imagery, and my friend's, and mine and Peter Blake's are all different.

I wonder how the widow Ogmore-Pritchard looked to Dylan Thomas. Did he have someone in mind? An old aunt. A landlady.

We make our way along the linear narrative, and get caught behind an old couple. They are scanning the love letters between Mog Edwards and Miss Myfanwy Price. He can't read Blake's writing, and is half deaf. She reads them aloud to him, he says 'What?' She reads them again, louder, her voice rising as her lips move closer to his ear. He cocks his head towards her.

'... I see you got a mermaid in your lap ...'

'What?'

A couple of teenagers giggle. They are on a school trip. An art class, I think. They are sketching in their wide, magnolia-paged books, and I imagine the essays that will be handed in, the class discussions, the blank stares and empty pages.

The attendant in his National Museum Cardiff uniform offers us leaflets and unwanted information. He points at the beginning and I nod politely. Yes, I'll take one in Welsh, please.

He must know every illustration by now. Does he take time to look every day? Does he see something new every time? Does he go home at night and dream about Mae Rose-Cottage drawing circles in lipstick around her nipples, or the watercolour of Mrs Willy Nilly's naked bottom as her husband smacks her over his knee? Don't spank me, please, teacher.

He tells us that at two o'clock they will play Richard Burton's reading of the play. I imagine his voice like a thick cloud spreading under the ceiling of the gallery. The story trickling down over the listener. Now also a viewer. People moving from image to image following the tread and nodding in agreement.

All day people enter and exit. Like the people in Llareggub, who watch each other and pass judgement, we look in on their lives. See familiarities, recognise people, places and feelings.

Like a dream within a dream, I watch people looking at, and analysing, a visual representation of someone's imagined version of someone else's written documentation of his imagination. It's beautiful, abstract and absurd. As the layers are slowly peeled back, at the heart of everything, lies obsession and desire. Both Dylan Thomas and Peter Blake obsessed over the little fishing town, its people and their dreams and desires.

For Thomas the story slowly went from a labour of love to a ticking deadline, but for Blake it was a source of escapism and enjoyment. The infernally, eternally unfinished project was forced to end for Thomas, but for Blake it still goes on. He continues to listen to the play weekly, he still illustrates the dreams and doings of Thomas's villagers.

At the museum, walking from drawing to drawing, watercolour to collage, I wonder what Thomas is telling me. Of Blake's work it's the collages that work wonders in my imagination. Glimpses of the familiar cut and pasted together illustrate the layers of *Under Milk Wood*, and stay true to Blake's own artistic vision and style. The dreams in the story seem to all be the secret desires of the dreamers. Is that what they are to Thomas? Dreams. A window into our secret longings.

The village is small and at times insular. If you know Wales you can nod in appreciation and recognition at the quirky names and descriptions. But really, change the name of the town and the people, and could it not be anywhere? It's a comment of the never-changing and enduring human condition. We keep dreaming, hoping, desiring and obsessing.

Thomas is said to have called *Under Milk Wood* a reaction to the bombings of Hiroshima. Reminding people of the beauty in the world.

Humanity, with all its petty faults and habits, is still beautiful and exciting and interesting no matter who or where we are, and no matter what happens to us.

I imagine this is what trapped Peter Blake. Depicting humanity with all its quirks, tenderness, absurdity and strength. Being able to visually show what's inside a person. What makes them wake up in the morning and continue another day. Let life keep moving. *Under Milk Wood* was a ready made microcosm of a world. Ready for him to dig into and explore.

The teenagers have left the museum. Loud and happy. 'The boys are dreaming wicked,' Peter Blake writes under a collage of cowboys, escapism and scantily clad girls, and I hope they are.

The old couple are by the exquisite watercolour portrait Blake has painted of Dylan Thomas. It hangs just as you enter. Cigarette in mouth, pen in hand, the cuffs of his shirt undone, and with a furrowed brow, the painter captures the writer in a moment of creativity. It is a warm, affectionate, honest, thoughtful depiction. A reminder that art is work, dedication and desire. It consumes, inspires and drives you towards a destination that may or may not exist.

A short distance form the National Museum Cardiff, at The Martin Tinney commercial gallery, another collection of work inspired by Thomas is exhibited. Here it is Ceri Richards, one of Wales's leading mid twentieth-century artists, whose paintings and prints are hung on the white walls of the light, spacious gallery.

In the early 1940s, having already begun experimenting with surrealism, something in Dylan Thomas's poems resonated in Richards and he started the first of many works inspired by his poetry. Work that would continue, with oil paintings, lithographs and drawings, until his death in 1971.

There was something in Thomas's words that inspired Richards to produce some of his most beautiful and haunting work. A common experience of the horrors of the Second World War was the catalyst, but it was a shared view of the brutality and cyclical heart of the natural environment as a metaphor for humanity that stoked the fire of creativity. An obsession with the contrast of light and darkness, life and death, and with what we as human beings are capable of in terms of both good and evil. Though neither Thomas nor Richards experienced the Swansea Blitz in 1941 at first hand it strongly affected both of them, and as a result their work. After visiting the ruins of the city Dylan Thomas said 'our Swansea is dead', and during the next few years he would write some of his darkest and most emotional poetry.

As with Thomas, Richards' response was an emotional one. Venturing further into surrealism, inspired by the work of Kandinsky and Picasso, his work became bleaker and more forceful, and though not directly political the reverberation of the general zeitgeist of fear and anticipation is tangible.

In 1953 Ceri Richards went to The Boat House in Laugharne to meet Thomas. The connection was instant, and when Thomas died, less than a month later, Richards felt he had lost a kindred spirit and started working on a series of paintings directly inspired by the *Collected Poems* of the writer. Throughout the 1950s and '60s, Richards continued to paint his responses to Thomas's poetry, and these paintings are without doubt among his most beautiful and haunting. The critical highlight of this era is probably the collection of twelve prints from 1965 entitled *Twelve Lithographs for Six Poems by Dylan Thomas*, also known as the Dylan Thomas suite.

In silence and with the rooms of the gallery bathed in light I slowly take in the scale of the work.

I step backwards, the sound of my footsteps on the light wooden floor, to fully appreciate 'the force that through the green fuse drives the flower'. A large oil painting, hung as the heart of the exhibition. In the next room, surrounded by the twelve lithographs that make up the Dylan Thomas suite, I stand in the middle of the room and the effect is eerie. In the light and stillness the prints seem even more aggressive and apocalyptic. Nature is violent and forceful, and life, death and humanity is part of the eternal cycle. Twisted bodies, limbs, grabbing hands, skulls, owls and crashing dark waters are entwined with roses and seeds shaped likes breasts and vaginas to remind us that in the middle of fear, death and darkness is life and beauty.

I turn to the right, and in the middle of all the darkness and death is a small oasis of light and humour.

Shortly before his death in 1971 Ceri Richards drew nine portraits of characters from *Under Milk Wood*, and the mood could not be in starker contrast to the other work. The nine prints hang together so they can all be taken in at the same time. The faces are open, and the depictions are light, playful and tender.

Captain Cat sits quietly in his chair with his big coat and captain's cap, hands folded on his walking cane. Polly Garter is on her knees scrubbing the floor, her face bright and smiling. The children are playing after school's out, a light drawing of pure happiness and freedom.

I look at Blake's early illustrations of the *Under Milk Wood* dreams, and I look at two artists, Blake and Thomas, at the beginning of their careers.

I think about the love and dedication that must be there to devote yourself so completely to one project. The frustration that must also be felt, when trying to aim for a goal that just doesn't get any closer. How there is always something to change, make better, and how there is always a new idea and thought that throws you off course and opens new and unexpected doors.

I think about my own work, and how new this level of commitment makes me feel. I wonder if I will ever experience it, and I find myself hoping I don't. In so many ways it must be a millstone.

With Richards the connection to Thomas's work was emotional. A shared viewpoint, shared fears and a similar experience. He articulated something Richards felt, and it compelled him to visualise it.

I love the freedom of creating. Imagining myself the master of my fate. But like in Llareggub, as with Thomas's deadline, the clock is always ticking. Even with freedom, art and creativity there is urgency, desire, deadlines and the circles of routine.

Like Utah Watkins, Mae Rose Cottage and Organ Morgan in Llareggub we all wake up in the morning from our dreams and desires, and take them with us. They shape who we are and what we do.

Dylan Thomas, Peter Blake and Ceri Richards all showed the world their obsessions, and through their art we look through a window into their desires. A need to create, depict, explain and make sense of the beauty, fears, desire and enduring absurdity of the human condition.

O Rare Dylan Thomas:
A Book-Dealer's View

Jeff Towns

This is not a scholarly bibliographical essay, it is rather the self-indulgent ramblings and selected memories of a bookseller who is approaching a half century in Wales, coupled with a specific, maybe obsessional pursuit of the original manuscripts, letters, books, ephemera and iconography of Dylan Thomas, across the Western World.

Dylan Thomas has been well served by his bibliographers. The standard bibliography, *Dylan Thomas: A Bibliography*, was compiled by J. Alexander Rolph (himself a bookseller). It was published by J.M. Dent (Dylan's publishers) in 1956 with a foreword by Dame Edith Sitwell. Rolph had begun work on it in 1952 while Dylan was still alive; the book reproduces a letter from Thomas in response to Rolph's request for his help. Dylan refers to the idea of the book as both a 'fantastic project' and a 'peculiar cause'. Needless to say Dylan was no great keeper of records and could offer scant assistance. He prophesies thus: 'I must warn you I can't remember much.'

Indeed, letters from Dylan to Rolph have Dylan asking Rolph for assistance in finding elusive printings of stories for inclusion in a new anthology. The great achievement of Rolph's bibliography is that it actually manages to be a good read. It is well laid out and clearly printed, has sixteen good plates, and offers a slightly eccentric methodology, in as much as Rolph's first section, his 'A' items, is comprised of very detailed 'Literary biographies' of the published poems written by Dylan Thomas from September 1933 [London]-1956'. This section in particular makes very interesting reading and the succeeding sections on the Books, Periodicals and Anthologies are full of useful information. The book ends with short sections on Translations and Gramophone recordings. All the entries are presented with very full bibliographical descriptions and details of print runs, reprints and sales are also included wherever such figures were available.

More recently, but still over forty years ago, Ralph Maud one of the pathfinders of Dylan Thomas scholarship and exegesis published his *Dylan Thomas in Print; a Bibliographical History*. It was published first in the States and a year later it appeared in the UK [1970/71]. This book offers an encyclopaedic listing of books and magazines by and about Dylan Thomas. It does not attempt to provide the bibliographical detail that Rolph offers, but it is more than just a checklist because scattered throughout the listings, both in the main body of the text and in footnotes, it reprints interesting articles and reviews by and about Dylan, many of which had been hitherto hard to find.

A few years ago Ralph Maud asked me to collaborate with him on a new edition of Rolph but the project came to nought, in many respects because Rolph did such a good job. Between them these two pioneer bibliographers of Thomas did not miss very much at all. The only significant addition to these two works is the *Author Checklist* distributed by an American Bookselling company – Quill and Brush run by Pat and Alan Aherne and their daughters. They recently approached me to help update the Dylan Thomas Checklist and much of what I write about here is contained in the most recent list they have published

But before I begin my parade of Dylan Thomas rarities and curiosities a word about Dylan Thomas's bibliography in general. Dylan Thomas's canon is not vast – just seven or eight lifetime books and perhaps a dozen significant posthumous books. This is perhaps doubled by the American variants. His *Collected Poems 1934-1952* contains under a hundred poems, but his juvenilia, fragments and notebook poems may just about double that number. Add to this a couple of dozen short stories, an unfinished novel, some thirty radio scripts, twenty film scripts and top this body of work off with *Under Milk Wood* – and there you have it – not too vast an output to trouble bibliographers about except for two related coincidences. Firstly, Dylan was writing during the golden age of the literary periodical – Connolly's *Horizon*, Eliot's *Criterion*, 'Life and Letters', Grigson's *New Verse*, Keidrych Rhys's *WALES*, Tambimuttu's *Poetry London*, Roger Roughton's surrealist *Contemporary Poetry and Prose*, and short-lived curiosities like *Seven* and *Yellow Jacket*.

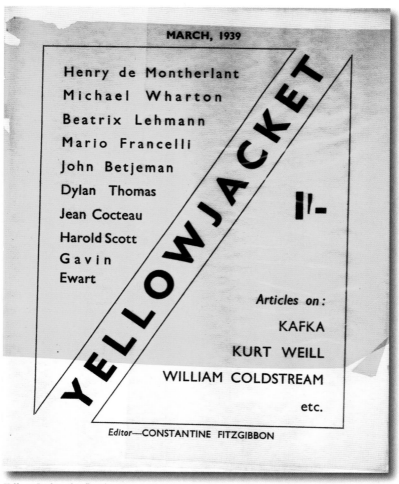

Yellow Jacket, the first issue actually sported a yellow cellophane over-wrapper.

These were all UK Publications; add to them their American equivalents – *Poetry* from Chicago, James Laughlin's *New Directions in Poetry and Prose*, *The Partisan Review* and the numerous University based periodicals such as *The Kenyon Review*, and *The Swanee Review*. And then there were the more exotic foreign publications – Henry Miller's 'Delta' and Eugene Jolas' surrealist *Transition* – in the Fall issue, 1936, Dylan has a poem, 'Then was Ny Neophyte' and his short story 'The Mouse and the Woman' – the cover is by Miro.

YTransition,a couple of poems by Thomas, the cover by Miro.

The thirties and the forties – the two decades, which encompass almost all of Dylan's publishing life, were also the heydays of good quality literary periodicals. The wartime paper shortage and the development of Television contributed to their eventual but quite dramatic demise. Maud lists over 100 little mags that published Dylan. So there existed for Dylan this vast opportunity and marketplace for poems and short stories which he endeavoured to exploit to the full which leads to my second observation.

After his short spell as a tyro journalist on his local paper, Dylan never had a proper job with regular hours and a regular salary – he lived by his pen. And it was hard going and he was constantly short of money to keep himself and then his wife and three children. He clutched at any source of income and he submitted stuff and constantly badgered editors. Moreover he was not beyond offering the same poem or story to more than one editor. As a result almost all his individual poems or stories appear first in at least one periodical and often two, then in an anthology before coming out in one of his own books – at least three bites of the cherry for Dylan and three bibliographical references for us. Throw into this mix the curious anomaly, in that, although Dylan described himself thus: 'I am a painstaking conscientious, involved and devious craftsman in words,' and that he was poet who constantly worked and reworked his poems in draft after draft; once he gave up his poems up to an editor he was quite cavalier about proofing and misprints. Thus the same poem often never appears the same way twice. Many of these variations may be minutiae of punctuation – but even these can be crucial, and sometimes, whole words are mutated and changed. This makes for rich pickings for bibliographers, librarians, booksellers and collectors.

This can be shown quite deftly if we look closely at the publishing saga of one poem – his early and famous poem, 'Light breaks where no sun shines'. It is poem A.8 in Rolph and Maud tells us in his masterly editions of *Dylan Thomas; The Notebook Poems* (1967 and 1989) that this poem was written in his fourth notebook in November of 1933. [This boastful bookseller cannot resist mentioning that he once had in his possession Dylan Thomas's ink-stained and scruffy School Physics

Exercise Book, labelled on the upper cover 'D. M. Thomas 1V A'. It
dated from 1926 and in amongst the rough notes from a lecture on Light
I was delighted to discover these prescient and echoing lines;

> Light
> Light is invisible.
> Light travels in straight lines.

The exercise book is now part of the Dylan Thomas Collection at
the National Library of Wales.]

Dylan was obviously pleased with his notebook poem because it is
first published, without revisions, in *The Listener* in March 1934,
entitled 'Light'. It is worth noting that this publication led to Dylan
being noticed and approached by three of the doyens of the London
literary scene, Stephen Spender, Geoffrey Grigson and T. S. Eliot. Dylan
also boasted to Pamela Hansford Johnson, his current girlfriend, that
the poem's sexual imagery provoked sack-fulls of outraged and
complaining letters and that this led to the BBC banning any future
publication of his work. Although phrases such as 'Candle in the thighs'
and 'the fruit of man unwrinkling in the stars' are not devoid of sexual
references, his boasts are largely hyperbolic bravado for he was gracing
the pages of *The Listener* again in October of the same year and he went
on to become a regular contributor. The poem next appears in 1934 in
what was to become an annual anthology, *The Year's Poetry; A
Representative Selection*. It was compiled by Denys Kilham, Gerald
Gould and John Lehman. Rolph describes this publication as
constituting Dylan's first ever appearance in book form, and it is listed
as D.1 in his section 'Contributions by Dylan Thomas to books'
(however see my entry on *The Boy's Own Paper* below). Just a few days
after the appearance of *The Year's Poetry* in December of 1934, Dylan's
first book, the monumental *18 Poems*, was first published by *The
Sunday Referee* and Parton Street Bookshop.

They printed 500 sets of sheets but only 250 copies were bound up
as the first issue, the remaining sheets were bound up and published in
1936 and constitute the second issue. During these printings minor

changes to the text occur – 'glow-worms' loses the hyphen and 'fenced' gains a comma.

The poem next appears in Dylan's first American book *The World I Breathe* published by James Laughlin's New Directions in 1939, in an edition of just 700 copies. In 1942 a rogue publisher Reginald Caton rather dubiously obtained the rights of *18 Poems* and offered a series of reprints bearing the imprint of his The Fortune Press (each printing was dated 1934 and he went on issuing the book in variant bindings and colours until as late as 1954). The poem is finally included by Dylan in his *Collected Poems 1934-1952*, but by now the first line has become its title and 'glow-worms' has got its hyphen back! Along the way the poem also appears in a French translation in the magazine *Fontaine* in 1942, (only the second translation into French of a Dylan Thomas poem to appear), and later it was released as a recording both on an LP and as an EP. One poem; a variety of different incarnations, and so it is with so much of Dylan's out-put.

Much of the above – but not all, can be found in Rolph and Maud, but now to a few books, editions and curiosities that they missed, although some have appeared since they published.

Proof Copies

Rolph makes a generic comment regarding his attitude to 'Proof Copies' in his introduction to his Section B. – Books and Pamphlets by Dylan Thomas: 'Proof copies are not mentioned except where some special significance attaches to them, but they may be taken to exist in the case of all bound books except *18 Poems*.' This may be so, but he goes on to say that the 'quantity of such proofs can be reckoned at about thirty copies before and during the war and about double this figure thereafter'. This makes these fragile little paper covered productions very scarce and I believe that in many instances Rolph was not in a position to inspect certain proofs to decide whether or not they offered any 'special significance'. Herewith some observations on Thomas's *Proofs*.

TWENTY-THREE
POEMS

BY

DYLAN THOMAS

Advance Proofs Only

Rolph B. Maud, unrecorded Proof copy of *Twenty-Three Poems.*

Neither Rolph nor Maud makes mention of any proofs for *Twenty-Five Poems* Dylan's first book with a major and his lifetime publisher J.M. Dent. Rolph does describe Dylan showing his first publisher, Victor Neuberg, a sheaf of twenty-one poems. Neuberg was eager to cash in on the responses to *18 Poems* and suggested that Dylan make up the number of poems to twenty-five. At this point Dylan was taken on by a mainstream publisher and it was indeed *Twenty-Five Poems* that Richard Church of J.M. Dent & Sons saw through the press in 1936. Rolph makes no mention of the proof of this book, but close examination of my copy of a proof (Now in the National Library of Wales) shows that the first section of the book was entirely reset before publication. The proof copy has no dedication page, which in the published version is simply to Caitlin, this was, after all, Dylan's first book since his marriage. In the proof copy the second contents page, lists only six of the seven stories listed in the published book, – no mention of 'The Enemies'. However, this story is to be found in the text. Once into the text proper, in the proof the first poem is entitled 'January 1939' with no number. In the published version this poem is number one, with 'January 1939' below, and in parenthesis. In the proof the second poem – 'I make this warring absence' is poem number one, but it is split so that poem number two begins with the line 'These once blind eyes have breathed'. This is reflected in the contents page of the proof. In the published version of the book this poem has disappeared from the contents page and has become part of poem two, 'I Make This Warring Absence'. From then on the poems and numbers are identical.

Collected Poems 1934-1952 An unrecorded proof
Rolph writes:

> *A few weeks prior to publication 68 proof copies were printed; these have the leaves which ultimately bore the 'Authors Prologue' blank except for the word 'Preface' on p. (v), also the dedication and the 'Note' on its verso are lacking (pp. (v)-(vi) in the trade edition)'*

We have what appears to be a later, unrecorded proof, almost certainly not one of the original sixty-eight copies. This proof has an extra fascicle inserted after the preface which has the 'Authors Prologue' printed across a two-page opening. On 10 September 1952,

COLLECTED POEMS 1934–1952
by Dylan Thomas

With a frontispiece portrait of the author
by AUGUSTUS JOHN, *and a ~~Preface~~ by the Author*

Demy 8vo.   12*s*. 6*d*. net   `˅Prologue in Verse.`

Special edition of sixty-five numbered copies, signed by the author, of
which sixty are for sale; mould-made paper, leather binding; £5 5s. net

Mr. Dylan Thomas is one of the most widely discussed poets of his
generation, and the place of his work in the field of modern poetry
is assured. This volume gathers together all his published poems,
including those from books which have been out of print for a while,
that is to say from *Eighteen Poems* (1934), *Twenty-five Poems* (1936),
The Map of Love (1939), which contained sixteen poems as well as seven
stories, and *Deaths and Entrances* (1946), which was among the few
modern writings included in the Festival of Britain great books exhibition at the Victoria and Albert Museum.   In addition the present
volume includes ten new poems which have not hitherto appeared in
book form, and the author has written a ~~preface~~ for it. `Prologue in Verse`
   In 1939, Mr. Herbert Read, reviewing the poems in *The Map of*
Love, wrote: 'They contain the most absolute poetry that has been
written in our time, and one can only pray that this poet will not be
forced in any way to surrender the subtle course of his genius.' Since
then Dylan Thomas has still further increased his reputation, and his
output to the present time is consolidated in this important volume.

★ *Probable publication date:* NOVEMBER 1952
4

(just one month before publication of *Collected Poems*) Dylan writes a
letter to E.F. Bozman, his editor at Dent in which he includes 'The
Prologue', and tries to explain it, 'I intended to write ... a more-or-less
straightforward and intimate prose preface, and then funked it. And then
I began to write a prologue in verse ... To begin with, I set myself,
foolishly perhaps, a most difficult task: The Prologue is in two verses
in my manuscript a verse to a page of fifty-one lines each. And the
second verse rhymes backward with the first ... Why I acrosticked
myself like this, don't ask me' And he asks quite pointedly: 'I will have
a proof of this, won't I?'

   In this later proof the printing of 'Prologue' follows Dylan's two-
page original typescript in which the central couplet spans the page
break:

Sheep white Hollow farms
To Wales in my arms

It is also printed with line numbers in the margins, in fives, advancing to fifty and then descending from fifty. All this helps the reader detect this complicated pattern. I am sure that after struggling with such a challenge, 'It has taken the devil of a time to finish', wrote Dylan, he wanted his readers to notice his achievement. Furthermore a new 'Note' in this proof explains this structure to us: 'It is in two verses of fifty one lines each, and the second verse rhymes backward with the first.' However this was not to be. To squeeze the poem across two pages a much smaller typeface was necessary, which was almost unreadable, and typographically unpleasant. In the published version it has become the 'Author's Prologue' and it is printed over four pages without line numbering, and we are left to fathom out the rhyme scheme by ourselves because the 'Note' from the proof is also scrapped. In the new note, we are given no clues as the Prologue's intricacies but we are told: 'These poems with all their crudities, doubts, and confusions, are written for the love of Man and in praise of God, and I'd be a damn' fool if they weren't.' In both proofs 'Paper and Sticks' is still printed on page 116, but the letter to Bozman, quoted above, ends with a footnote: 'Proof-reading the *Collected Poems*, I have the horrors of 'Paper & Sticks' on page 116. It's awful. I suppose it's quite impossible to cut it out? I shd so like it, somehow, to be omitted.'

Dylan got his wish because this poem had to go to accommodate the four pages of 'Prologue'. 'Do not go gentle into that good night' is moved from page 174 in the proofs, to page 116, somewhat compromising the rough chronological order of the poems. My copy also has an interesting printed publicity blurb pasted to the verso of the front wrapper, which has two identical corrections in Dylan's hand that indicates the real importance he placed on this new poem. In both cases 'Preface' is changed to 'Prologue in Verse', '... the author has written a preface (crossed out) for it. Prologue in Verse [added]

Poetry of Our Times. Being a Compilation of Modern Poetry together with some of its Ancestors, Thoth Bookshop Cairo, 1943. Not in Rolph or Maud.

A Chronology of curiosities

A small paperback in printed wrappers seems to have been aimed at both literate soldiers and ex-patriates. It appears to be edited by Eric de Nemes; the one page preface is signed E.N., and the book begins with a curious surrealist text 'Escape and Fall' described as 'A Ballad in Seven Drawings by Eric de Nemes'. The anthology begins with Donne ends with Watkins via Blake and the Romantics and most of the Moderns. It contains four poems by Dylan – 'Light breaks...' (yet again), 'On a Wedding Anniversary', 'Deaths and Entrances' and 'The

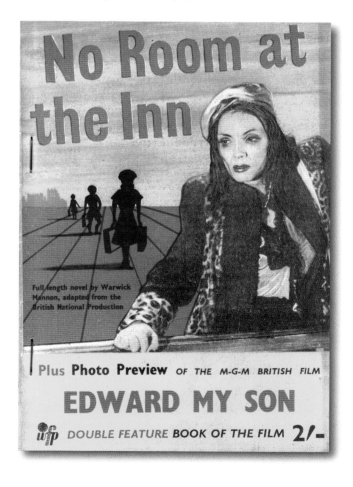

Force that Through the Green Fuse Drives ... the Flower...'

Printed paper wrappers feature stills from the film profusely illustrated with many stills inside. Dylan does not make the cover but is acknowledged on the title-page. Not in Rolph and although Maud lists

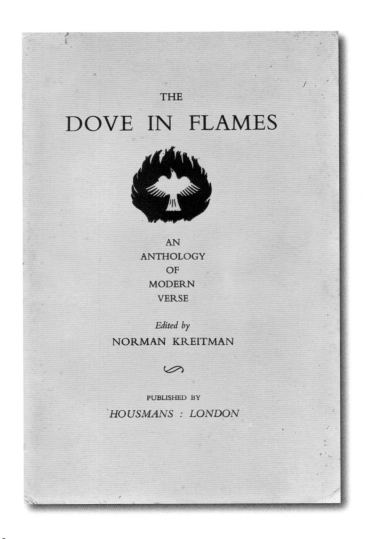

three references to reviews of this film he does not record this book's publication.

There is an unrecorded, small yellow booklet in paper wrappers. An anthology of war poems, it contains Dylan's two great Second World War poems – 'The Hand that Signed the Paper Felled a City' and 'A Refusal to Mourn the Death, by Fire of a Child in London'.

Among other poets represented are Ruthven Todd, e.e. cummings, Alun Lewis and David Gasgoyne. My copy has an inscription from the editor: 'To Dylan Thomas in admiration and with warmest wishes Norman Kreitman. Dec.1952.'

Unrecorded in the bibliographies Dylan did however write a letter to a G.F. Hench (?) from Majoda in New Quay in 1945 in which he grants permission for the use of these two poems in an Anthology to be

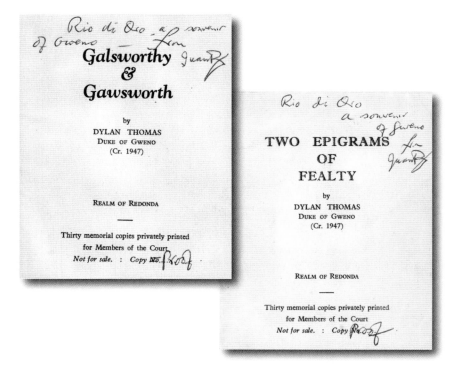

called *Poems for Europe* which in all probability was taken over by Kreitman and published here as *The Dove in Flames*.

Both Privately printed for members of the Court of Redonda in an edition of thirty numbered copies. Redonda is the mythical kingdom created by the writer M. P. Shiel and continued at this time by his successor John Gawsworth (the pseudonym of Terence Ian Fytton Armstrong). Gawsworth had bestowed the title 'Duke of Gweno' on Dylan Thomas when he admitted to the society in 1947. Maud does lists these and reprints Gawsworth's account of how he came to publish these two very insignificant short poems, one about, and one for John Gawsworth. My copies are presentation copies from Gawsworth to Wrey Gardiner of the Grey Walls Press. In 2003 to commemorate the fiftieth anniversary of Dylan's death I compiled, with the bookseller Arthur Freeman a pamphlet reprinting the two little poems and Arthur's account of his dealings with the nefarious Galsworthy. It was published by Tŷ Llên, Swansea.

A very rare etched poem
The etching opposite is from an exceedingly rare portfolio of *21 Etchings and Poems*. The edition comprised fifty numbered copies with 12 proof sets. It was conceived by the New York artist Peter Grippe in 1951 when he took over as director of Atelier 17 in its New York incarnation from S.W. Hayter the influential English artist (and sometime acquaintance of Dylan Thomas). Grippe chose Dylan Thomas as his poet to work with. The project brought together in all twenty-one modern artists and poets. The artists included many of the current New York school but most importantly the suite contains the only etching ever made by William de Kooning. The poets included many of Dylan's New York friends - William Carlos Williams, Theodore Roethke, Peter Viereck, David Lougee, George Reavey, Richard Wilbur, Frank O'Hara, Harold Norse and Herbert Read. Atelier 17 was disbanded in New York in 1954 but Grippe continued to work with the artists to bring the work to a conclusion. Eventually Morris Weisenthal (one of the poets involved) opened as a gallery – The Morris Gallery – and they finally produced the portfolio in 1960. This from the original press release:

This etching project, possibly the first of its kind in the
United States, joined two creative disciplines – art and
poetry. Poets and artists invited for this historic collaboration worked in the almost forgotten tradition of the Book of
Kells and William Blake's illuminated poems. Each print
closely integrates text and image, including a poem written
in the hand of its author and imagery created through a wide
range of innovative print techniques by an artist. For the
poets who transferred their poems, in their own handwriting,
onto the copper plate, this was an arduous, but exhilarating
experience; a slip of tool meant beginning anew as they
wrote backwards from a mirror image.

I have never owned nor even had a chance to acquire one of the Thomas/Grippe etchings – I do have an original prospectus that illustrated just one of the etchings and for this chooses Dylan's great anti-war poem. And I have two fifty-year-old booksellers' catalogues dating from 1964 when a proof set were offered by a great New York Bookselling firm The House of El Dieff, Inc at $3250 and, for me a heart rending duplicated book catalogue from about the same time from another New York dealer offering a proof of the Thomas etching at $200.They begin their description 'AN EXTRAORIDNARY THOMAS ITEM and end it: 'Here is a unique opportunity to acquire a Thomas item of the first magnitude.' Where is the Tardis when you most need it?

And finally a more recent, irreverent, ephemeral piece of Dylan Thomas Iconography – part inspiration, part perspiration.

The Poet On My Shoulder

George Tremlett

Dylan Thomas has been leaning over my shoulder for over sixty years, informing my daily search for words; helping me find the right ones for every occasion – whether to make a point, catch the ear, or flesh out the substance of an otherwise dull argument.

Words, words, words – yes, it's always been down to words.

'First, love the words', he said, and I have known exactly what he meant ever since I was first introduced to him by my English teacher at King Edward VI School, Stratford upon Avon.

At the time the thought that mine might have been an unusual childhood never occurred to me. Life, as Lennon said, is what happens to us while we are busy making other plans – and my plans had been chosen for me, to qualify for the Royal Veterinary College in Edinburgh, where I would follow in my grandfather's footsteps, before joining his practice at Tarvin, serving the cattle farms across the Cheshire Plain and deep down into Wales as far as Machynlleth, for Bill Kendrick was a Welshman and so, in my heart, am I.

And that's another funny thing about my affinity with Thomas: his Welshness, for he neither wrote nor spoke in Welsh, tended to avoid those who do, and chose to centre his life in that one eccentric little corner of West Wales, Laugharne, where Welshness runs deep but the language is hardly ever spoken – and, so far as we can tell, never has been.

*

Now back to school.

We learned English and performed school plays in the half-timbered, thick planked early Tudor rooms in which Shakespeare was taught Greek and Latin; his birthplace, the Church where he was baptised and buried, the house where he died and what was then called the Shakespeare Memorial Theatre were all just a few minutes' walk away. The school's ties with the theatre were close. We were given free tickets for every dress rehearsal and had a free run of the theatre wardrobe when choosing costumes for our school plays. From 1952-57, I saw every production at the Memorial Theatre in the days of Laurence Olivier, Vivien Leigh, John Gielgud, Michael Redgrave, Peggy Ashcroft and Anthony Quayle, often going back two or three times a season to see particular plays, sitting right up in the upper balcony, like a bat in the rafters.

My English teacher, Mr Wood, told us we really ought to absorb more contemporary writers, as well, and introduced us to Auden, Spender, George Barker, T.S. Eliot, and C. Day Lewis, most of whose poems left me cold; but then Wood read Dylan Thomas aloud, and that was when it all began... you really have to hear Dylan Thomas to know what he's all about; he wrote for the ear.

I remember listening to Thomas's radio talks, staying up late to watch him read 'A Story' (now better known as 'The Outing'), live on BBC TV just after the Coronation (like millions of other families we had just acquired our first TV), and buying *John O'London's Weekly* that week to read the only profile of Thomas written during his lifetime, Mimi Josephson's *Poet at the Boat House*.

The memories are vivid, for they were exciting times. Young men of my age were expecting to be called up for National Service, and Britain always seemed to be at war, often for reasons that made little sense – in Malaya, Korea, Cyprus or Kenya – and I had no wish to kill anyone. Most of us were far more interested in the American music that was coming into our homes via the ports and Radio Luxembourg, and for me that was especially true once all my plans had gone awry.

My grandfather died suddenly, without leaving a will. His assistant took over the practice, and my career path evaporated. My father decided to use a small inheritance to launch himself as a music hall promoter (he was convinced that television would not last!), and so my mid-teens were spent following Shakespeare and Dylan Thomas, playing rugby... and seeing every touring variety show, just at the time that music hall was dying, and the impresarios, who had toured the pre-War halls as hoofers, were now trying to save it by bringing in American stars like Johnnie Ray, Frankie Laine, The Platters, Tennessee Ernie

Ford, Guy Mitchell, Slim Whitman and even Laurel and Hardy. How could one ever forget sitting in the half-empty stalls at the Aston Hippodrome on a wet Monday night, watching Stan and Ollie performing against a backcloth of *The Lonesome Pine*?

And how could one forget Nat King Cole, Billy Eckstine, Mel Torme, Fats Domino, or the thrilling sound of early rock 'n' roll in the unlikely shape of Bill Haley and the Comets – or the new wave of British stars who suddenly found a national audience through television, like Alma Cogan, Frankie Vaughan, Shirley Bassey, Morecambe and Wise and Ken Dodd, who made me laugh until my stomach ached – and still does... followed by the likes of Tommy Steele, Cliff Richard and the Shadows, Marty Wilde, Billy Fury, Dickie Pride and Johnny Gentle, whose names we all knew, a whole generation of grammar school boys absorbing music and Thomas without knowing each other.

It's strange how influences fuse so easily. Although I did not succeed him, I owed much to my grandfather. His father died young and his mother ran a sweetshop at Lavister Rossett, near Wrexham; through scholarships, he won places at grammar school in Chester and the Royal Dick in Edinburgh; he married a vet's daughter, one of the Storrars, before joining the Royal Army Veterinary Corps during the First World War, to look after the horses in Turkey in those early days when the Generals thought the cavalry would win.

By the time I knew him, Grandad was in his early Fifties and I became the son he never had, which put rather a strain on the rest of the family. He taught me to read extensively, study history and politics, explore the structure of words and identify birds, flowers and trees. When my hopes of becoming a cattle vet disappeared, I decided to become a writer and learn what Thomas called his craft or sullen art just as he did, not by going to University but by finding a job as a junior reporter on a local evening newspaper – Thomas began his career on the *South Wales Evening Post* in Swansea; mine commenced on *The Coventry Evening Telegraph*, with four years in the newsroom and on the sub-editors' desk, learning how to handle words with accuracy.

More than that, the hard skills of daily journalism teach you to question every piece of information. My news editor taught me that every story should satisfy the reader, which could be best achieved by repeating the mantra, 'Who, what, why, where, when and how are my best friends' every time I sat down at a typewriter... and sometimes stood at my elbow shouting 'Where?' as I struggled to reach a deadline with the latest shoplifting news from Coventry Magistrates' Court.

No one in the *Telegraph* newsroom earned more than £20 a week in 1957, and my salary as a trainee was £3 (which came down to £2 12s 8d after tax), so I supplemented my earnings by contributing news and features to any newspaper or magazine that would buy them – from *The Shields Gazette* to the *Leicester Mercury*, *The Co-operative News*, *Meat Trade Weekly*, *Club Secretary*, *Chemist & Druggist*, *Drapers' Record* and, of course, the weekly newspaper that became my generation's bible, *The New Musical Express*, as their Midlands correspondent.

Either for the *Telegraph* or *NME*, I covered every touring music show between 1957 and 1961 in both Coventry and Birmingham – from rock 'n' roll to jazz, gospel, folk and rhythm 'n' blues, ranging from Chris Barber, Lonnie Donegan and Lyttleton through to the legendary and previously unseen American musicians who were now being allowed to perform in Britain with the lifting of the Musicians' Union ban, including Count Basie and his Orchestra and Duke Ellington. I was still hitch-hiking back to Stratford to keep up with Shakespeare, and reading every new book on Thomas, especially his own *Quite Early One Morning* (1954), *A Prospect of the Sea* and *Adventures* (both 1955), *Dylan Thomas in America* by John Malcolm Brinnin (also 1955), *Leftover Life to Kill* by Caitlin Thomas (1957), *Letters to Vernon Watkins* (also 1957), *Dylan Thomas: The Legend and the Poet* by E.W. Tedlock (1960) and *Four Absentees* by Rayner Heppenstall (also 1960).

The books left me wanting to know more, never answering the questions who, what, why, where, when and how, especially Caitlin's, which was a scream of pain without any deeper explanation.

*

As soon as my apprenticeship ended, armed with a certificate from The National Council for the Training of Journalists and a £100 loan from the manager of Martin's Bank, I caught the train to London to become a freelance writer. It was a foolhardy thing to do, really, but I had read *Adventures in the Skin Trade* and knew my destination. That was in 1961, the year I last received a weekly wage, living instead on regular work for the *NME*, Saturday shifts on Sunday newspapers, helping to produce house journals, and syndicating features on British rock 'n' roll to the music papers that began to flourish in Holland, Germany, Sweden, Norway, Finland, the United States and Japan from late 1962 onwards in the wake of The Beatles, The Who and the Rolling Stones and all those who followed – Cream, Queen, Led Zeppelin and the like.

I had never wanted to play music any more than write poetry or play guitar. My interest was in who made the music and why, and what they were trying to say, just as my interest in Thomas lay in trying to understand the influences that formed him, his character and achievement.

For sixteen years, my work as a rock 'n roll writer funded a career in London government, led to me writing eighteen rock 'n' roll biographies (and two more that remain unpublished), and gave me time to indulge myself in Dylan Thomas, reading everything written about him, absorbing his recorded poems, hearing his words in theatre in whatever form. As members of The Dylan Thomas Society my wife and I met his contemporaries and family, usually in the very same room at the Sesame Club where Thomas used to attend upon Edith Sitwell, and Jane became the society's secretary. Our companion at these events was often our close friend Eric Barton, who ran the Baldur Bookshop on Hill Rise in Richmond. We used to meet most mornings for coffee and croissants, and Eric always had some new story to tell for he was the first bookseller to specialise in Thomas's works, letters and manuscripts, knew many of the family's closest friends and campaigned for The Boat House in Laugharne to be preserved as a museum (which it has been, though largely because Caitlin inserted a covenant in the sale documents insisting that it was to be used for no other purpose).

Through Eric I learned of the simmering disputes that continued for over thirty years between Caitlin and the trustees of The Dylan Thomas Estate, and the contempt felt by the family and their closest friends for 'the Swansea Boys', that tiny circle of small town contemporaries who fed stories to his biographers, suggesting that they were Thomas's inspiration, and his life would not have ended so sadly had he not left Swansea or met his wife. It was all delusionary, and I have taken great care over the years not to be a part of it, having been warned who to avoid by Eric, Mervyn Levy, Fred Janes and Reggie Smith.

*

Having met through the Dylan Thomas Society, his daughter Aeronwy and I sat on the committees that raised the funds and planned the installation of the memorial plaque in Poets' Corner, Westminster Abbey, on 1 March 1982 with a replica later unveiled at St Martin's Church in Laugharne, where the Thomases' children were christened, and Dylan and Caitlin now lie together in the adjoining churchyard.

Until then it had never occurred to me to write about Thomas, any more than I would choose to analyse Shakespeare, Rodin or David Hockney, for the one enduring quality of all great art, no matter what form it takes, lies in its perfection. And, in my view, Thomas achieved perfection in poems like 'The Force That Through the Green Fuse Drives the Flower', 'After the Funeral', 'Light Breaks Where No Sun Shines', 'Fern Hill', 'Poem in October', 'In My Craft or Sullen Art', 'Do Not Go Gentle Into That Good Night', 'The Hand That Signed the Paper', 'And Death Shall Have No Dominion', his two War poems, 'Ceremony After a Fire Raid' and 'Among Those Killed In the Dawn Raid Was A Man Aged a Hundred', and perhaps a dozen more.

Only fools try to deconstruct perfection. D.H. Lawrence made the same point, saying one should never criticise a Modigliani, and that's how I feel about Thomas, whom I have come to know intimately through living in Laugharne, sharing my life with his people and their landscape, and writing *Caitlin: In A Warring Absence* with his widow (1986), *Dylan Thomas: In the Mercy of his Means* (1991) and *The Death of Dylan Thomas*, with the American neurosurgeon James Nashold (1997). I know exactly why Richard Burton chose to be buried with his copy of *The Collected Poems*, and why President Jimmy Carter keeps his on a bedside table, reading one or two poems every night before turning off the light. There is an intimate bond between us all, just as there was among the rock 'n' rollers, whether we were growing up in Liverpool, Lubbock, Hibbing or Penge. I sometimes think it may have something to do with *sound*, for it's listening to words and the sound of words accompanied by music that provides the link – and Bob Dylan, John Lennon, Mick Jagger, Eric Clapton, Paul McCartney, David Bowie and Marc Bolan have all acknowledged their debt to Thomas.

None of us knew what to expect at Westminster Abbey, for there were no formalities other than hymns and prayers, preceding the moment when Aeronwy stepped forward to remove the flag and reveal her father's memorial plaque, carved by Jonah Jones. We had no idea how many people would turn up, perhaps fifty or sixty we thought, but the Dean himself, Edward Carpenter, another keen Thomas fan, warned us to expect the unexpected... and 3000 people arrived, from many different parts of the world, united I believe in an act of communion, by the sound of one man's voice and his respect for words.

Afterwards we adjourned to the House of Lords for what turned into a crowded and very noisy reception where Jane and I found ourselves wedged in an alcove with Ted Hughes, who had travelled up from North Tawton, and one of Thomas's closest friends, Reggie Smith, the radio producer once suspected of organising a Communist cell within Broadcasting House. After talking about Devon, where we lived for the first six years of our marriage, just a few miles away from North Tawton, Hughes suddenly said: 'Have you read the biographies – aren't they dreadful?'

'I wouldn't speak to them,' said Smith, and we found ourselves in agreement about the Fitzgibbon and Ferris biographies, although I did put in a good word for Ackerman and Bill Read, who both wrote well of Thomas with few resources.

'Dylan can't have been the kind of man they say he was or he wouldn't have pulled it off... and we wouldn't be here today,' said Hughes, adding, 'Why don't you write about him? You've written about rock 'n' roll, and Dylan would have known what all that was about.'

Well, dear reader, I did – and now, approaching the last years of my own life, I find myself thinking more and more about Thomas's. My books were written for a purpose – *Caitlin* to explore their marriage (the narrative begins on the day they met and ends with his death); *Dylan* to redress the balance after the damage done by Brinnin, Fitzgibbon and Ferris, and *The Death of Dylan Thomas* to explain how a healthy young man in his prime had his life cut short by negligence, his own and other people's – and what happened thereafter with the formation of The Dylan Thomas Estate and Caitlin driven into exile.

There still has not been an all-embracing, comprehensive biography of Dylan Thomas and it may be too soon to write one; but I am thinking about it, knowing what his letters left unsaid, understanding how his appeal crosses all racial and religious boundaries, driven by thoughts of the kind of man I know he really was, blessed by what Caitlin always called a 'gift' and carrying that burden lightly, living without possessions, and depending solely on words; those damned, elusive words.

Dylan Thomas was not the kind of man you read about today in this, his Centenary year. He was warm, loving and gentle; a good son who cared for his parents in their fragility; a better husband and father than legends suggest; a socialist whose beliefs shaped his humility; a loyal friend; a man whose friends were often black, Jewish or Gay at a time when this was rare; a writer who conscientiously devoted himself to his craft, working to a daily routine; a man whose minor weaknesses mean very little when you look at his life as a whole.

The fascination of his life for me lies still in the who, what, why, where, when and how, and the fact (as I see it) that these all came together when he left Swansea, married Caitlin and found his spiritual home in Laugharne, writing much of his best work here and living, as he put it, 'off and on, up and down, high and dry, man and boy ... for fifteen years, or centuries, in this timeless, beautiful, barmy (both spellings) town, in this far, forgetful, important place of herons, cormorants (known here as billy duckers), castle, churchyard, gulls, ghosts, geese, feuds, scares, scandals, cherry-trees, mysteries, jackdaws in the chimneys, bats in the belfry, skeletons in the cupboards, pubs, mud, cockles, flatfish, curlews, rain, and human, often all too human beings.'

How could anyone not want to know more about a man who achieved such grace working within a vision like that?

Listen to the Music

Steve Groves

What would Igor Stravinsky have asked if you were to meet him? This is the man who changed the face of twentieth-century music with *Petrushka* and *The Rite of Spring* and *The Firebird*, so when the composer met Dylan Thomas for the first and only time at his hotel bedroom in Boston in May 1953, he inquired about the poet's favourite tunes. (He probably didn't say tunes, but you get the drift.)

Il Travatore, said Thomas. He presumably thought better than to have brought up his days of making-it-up-on-the-spot sound-scaping with his teenage mates, the fun they had with their front room orchestra at the Swansea home of his great friend and by now composer Daniel Jones.

Now this is the version he told Jones later. Yes, when Stravinsky asked for a musical reference, Thomas brought up *Il Travatore*. Perfect! Stravinsky was known to have been a big fan of Verdi. But was this version of events accurate, or was it a tale he knew his old friend Jones would delight in?

Because the last time Jones had heard Thomas enthuse about *Il Travatore* was when they retired to a London studio where the poet had played him a 78rpm recording of the opera. But with the speed lever stuck on maximum, the whole thing was an octave too high. So the Stravinsky story would have confirmed Jones's suspicion that if Thomas did have a musical bone in his body, it was very well hidden.

Another version of events suggests Thomas told Stravinsky that Puccini was the man. Stravinsky in his turn told Thomas to get into Mozart.

Thomas was there in response to Stravinsky's invitation to write a libretto for a newly commissioned opera, and it would have been a fresh and fairly lucrative adventure for him. Thomas thought it an easy job. But since that meeting any collaboration between musicians, composers and Thomas has had to rely only on the words he left behind. And there

Encounters with Dylan

has been learned debate for generations about the suitability of his poetry and prose for musical adaptation or inspiration. And it continues: new works have been commissioned this year. The great, the good and others will interpret the Thomas catalogue in their own way. But listen to Thomas reading his own work now and try not hearing a lyric tenor doing the job, or a jazz drummer shuffling behind him; he doesn't recite, he sings those poems, wraps us in charm and pace and beat. In that, he was musical and some of Thomas's work was always ripe for melodic collaboration. And some of those post-mortem associations have been great. But not all. Donovan beatniking or John Cale pulling Dylan into *The Falklands Suite*, Eli Jenkins' Prayer set to Troyte and sung by every male voice choir in Christendom, orchestral interpretations and jazz improv and choral settings. Take your pick. Dylan Thomas's work has been there to be quavered and time-signatured and paradiddled.

Dylan Thomas and composer Daniel Jones were the best of friends from childhood and were part of the Kardomah Boys legend. Thomas spent hours, days even, at the Jones' family house, Warmley, ten minutes walk from Cwmdonkin Drive. 'Music, or, to use a broader term, sound played a very important part in our Warmley life,' said Jones in *My Friend Dylan Thomas* in 1977. 'The fact that Dylan had no knowledge of music or musical skill was much more of an advantage than a disadvantage, because it ensured that anything we produced in concert would be unconventional.' Instruments played by any friends there included a piano, violins, cello, recorders and a biscuit tin percussion section. They invented composers and musicians such as Lacketty Apps and X.Q. Lumm. Dylan and Jones also devised 'chanting pieces'; compositions included *Badgers Beneath My Vest*.

In their early years Jones had set Thomas's work to music, all of it 'appallingly bad stuff'. However his later style became unsuitable for musical setting, Jones reckoned. But their long-talked of plans of collaborating on an opera (and they had even thought of a theme – 'winning of freedom from oppression') – hadn't led to anything at that point. So Jones would have been fascinated by talk of the Stravinsky job, perhaps thinking that if that got off the ground there might be a chance of the two pals working together. And you might excuse him for being a little sceptical.

It had all started when W.H. Auden introduced Stravinsky to Thomas's work, in New York in 1950. Thomas was being lauded on his American tour and Auden turned up late at Stravinsky's place, saying he'd just rescued Thomas from some caper or other. And after that Stravinsky started reading Thomas's work and Mrs Stravinsky – Vera – went to hear him read at the University of Illinois. And then the great film director Michael Powell had an idea of making a movie based on an episode in *The Odyssey*. He'd recruited Thomas as scriptwriter and asked Stravinsky if he'd contribute the music. But – and this will be familiar to students of Thomas's life – the money wasn't there and the project fell through.

It was another project which led to Stravinsky and Thomas meeting to talk about collaboration. Boston University was ready to commission a short operatic piece and Robert Craft, the Russian's collaborator and right-hand man, suggested Thomas as librettist. One account suggests Stravinsky wasn't well and was in bed and wearing a beret when Thomas arrived. Thomas was shorter than Stravinsky expected. The composer thought his guest looked as if he drank too much and noticed that his belly and backside were, well, prominent. But he recalled to Craft, 'As soon as I saw him I knew the only thing to do was to love him.' Thomas accepted a glass of whisky and the collaborators got down to business. Dylan said he'd heard on radio the premiere of Stravinksy's *The Rake's Progress*, with its libretto by Auden and Chester Kallman. Stravinsky and he discussed themes; love and communication after a nuclear apocalypse, said Dylan, survivors inventing a new language. A very beautiful idea, thought Stravinsky.

'Dear Mr Stravinsky', wrote Dylan later, 'I've been thinking a lot about the opera and have a number of ideas – good, bad, and chaotic. As soon as I can get something down on paper, I should, if I may, love to send it to you.' Then the plan was go to with Caitlin to the Stravinsky home in Hollywood, making it an extension of his 1953 winter tour of America. Thomas talked the commission over with Daniel Jones who warned that Stravinsky would not be an easy man to work with – he might be 'immovably obstinate'. With the warning ringing in his ears Thomas set off for America, but only got as far as New York. 'I wanted to compose with him an opera,' Stravinsky recalled. 'And I invited him here where we had to sketch this libretto for this opera. And I waited here. And I received a telegram that he was dead in New York. So no more opera. It was only regret of knowing somebody which was a wonderful poet. And I always have his poetry with me because I loved him very much. And so I composed a piece of music in his memory and was very sad. And I don't know if the music translated this sadness.'

Stravinsky said he cried when he heard that Thomas had died in November. Within three months he'd written his *In Memoriam Dylan Thomas*. Robert Craft conducted the premiere within the year. There were three movements all over in less than eight minutes – dirge-canons in prelude and postlude for four trombones and a string quartet, and a string quartet setting of 'Do Not Go Gentle' sung by a tenor. Craft said the form of Thomas's villanelle would have appealed to Stravinsky, not least for its many repetitions. The *Rage, rage* music is itself repeated four times, other interludes are repeated too. It is, says Stephen Walsh in *The Music of Stravinsky*, one of the most moving and most satisfying of all Stravinsky's shorter compositions.

Before Thomas left for America in 1953, Daniel Jones had played for the poet a recording of his Third Symphony. It wasn't that much later that Jones was driven to Southampton Docks to accompany his friend's body back to Wales. And then – while in American Stravinsky was working on his *In Memoriam Dylan Thomas* – Jones was working on his fourth symphony, commissioned for the 1954 National Eisteddfod in Ystradgynlais and was premiered there. It was subtitled *In Memory of Dylan Thomas*.

Jones had composed those beautiful, unusual folksie settings of the songs for *Under Milk Wood*. As far as Jones was concerned, these lyrics were atypical Thomas. He knew he was flying in the face of opinions much-held by others when he said he didn't think that most of Thomas's work lent itself to musical setting. So while Stravinsky wrote three small movements including the 'Do Not Go Gentle' setting, Jones completed his fourth symphony to Thomas's memory, calling on a lifetime's friendship. It closes with an adagio of 'great emotional depth' according to one reviewer, his 'most eloquent work' said an obituary. The critic Rob Barnett says the three movements have 'a sense of the epic, of the nostalgic and the tragic – the raw stuff of symphonies.' This was an elegiac composition of 'sadness and sombre restraint', described by the great Neville Cardus as a work of conviction 'with moments of dark and deeply felt musical feeling'. It may be Jones's finest work.

It couldn't have been more personal. Is it fanciful to hear a friend's life crammed into this symphony? Rage and generosity, pastoral and stormy, reflective, intuitive, speedy, risky, tenderness with an underlying threat of everything not quite making it? And a sweet violin and then plucked strings dying. Did anyone outside his family know Thomas better than Daniel Jones?

At least Stravinsky and especially Daniel Jones knew Thomas personally – in Stravinsky's case fleetingly, in Jones's case intimately. Other collaborators have had just the words. How they would have loved the chance to talk to Thomas, to discuss collaboration, an opportunity to bend Thomas's rules with official sanction.

Now, in 2014, John Metcalf is one such composer who wishes that he could share a frothy coffee in the Kardomah with Thomas. He's been completing a six year project to turn *Under Milk Wood* into an opera. Opera, he says, can only be collaboration between the composer and the librettist. So Metcalf has found himself second-guessing Thomas's intentions in a text which is part of Welsh DNA and which – as others have found – you mess with at your peril.

'You have the composer determining so much of sub-text and context and timing and pacing and even naff ideas about costumes,' Metcalf said as rehearsals for his opera continued. 'So basically the more help you can get on the collaborative side the better. If I were sitting here now with Thomas he would be much more famous, but in this particular form would depend at least as much on what I do as what he does.'

Metcalf has had to take evidence from the various drafts to assume some of Thomas's thinking about the way in which *Under Milk Wood* would have change if he'd had more time on it. Might Captain Cat have emerged as the narrator; would character confusion – for example between Gossamer Beynon and Rosie Probert – have been sorted? 'First Voice, for example: what does he do? And you've got no idea because he's not very concrete. What is concrete and fascinating for a composer, and an opera composer, is that it's about sound. And more it's about intimate sound; there's a sense of intimacy about radio. When I listened to radio as a youngster it was just for me – it was for an audience of one. For this musical piece the audience needs to provide the visual imagination in the same way it would as radio piece.'

It's a risk, of course – doing anything at all with *Under Milk Wood* is a risk. But there's an upside, especially for a work with comedy running through it. Familiarity with the libretto can only help in that, Metcalf believes, because opera with which people are not familiar is a very hard sell. Most audiences do not do their homework beforehand for the experience. Language is such a strong part of this piece that understanding it before it starts can only help.

The musicality of Thomas's words leap off the page, Metcalf agrees. Far from a hindrance, he sees that as an advantage. 'Sloeblack and slow back' – it's tough for an actor to pin down that pun and alliteration, but a composer can break it into sound-note-syllables to emphasise with pitch and rhythm. It's a gift.

Plenty of people have tried over the years to take elements of *Under Milk Wood* and add music; male voice choirs had been doing justice or villainy to Eli Jenkins's sunset poem at regular junctures since it was set to Arthur Henry Dyke Troyte's eighteenth-century chant. The English guitarist Stephen Goss has arranged some of the set pieces – Lilly Smalls' *Oh There's a Face...*, for example – for guitar and voice. Composer Thomas Hewitt Jones's suite for small ensemble called *Under Milk Wood* has been well received.

But the one musical adventure that used *Under Milk Wood* as its launch-pad and has become a classic is Stan Tracey's 1965 jazz suite 'inspired' by Thomas's work. Londoner Tracey was 'quite knocked out' with the original New York recording of the play for voices. He had the chance to record with his quartet and was looking for something to base some compositions on. While lying in bed ruminating, he remembered the work. He settled down with the book and a copy of the album his wife had brought home, jotted down ideas for titles and then wrote for the titles and the characters.

The original quartet recording opens with 'Cockle Row' which is strangely rather ordinary and straight-ahead – nice-enough, though. But then comes 'Starless and Bible Black' which takes the whole thing to a different plane altogether. It became a definitive moment in British jazz; 'Tracey's meditations on Dylan Thomas's radio play are now almost as iconic as the source material', said the *Penguin Jazz Guide*. The solo by tenor sax player Bobby Wellins on 'Starless and Bible Black' lifts it completely out of the ordinary – a romantic, elegiac and lyrical performance that demands attention.

And then we move into 'I Lost My Step in Nantucket' and suddenly we're on much more familiar Tracey territory – all heavy, percussive left hand piano and those New York influences of Monk and Ellington force through. Tracey liked the image of Dancing Williams and he tried to make the music reflect that – a sort of jaunty blues piece, he said. A name suggested a mood or rhythm of harmonic sequence to him. He got a feeling from the words and tried to reflect that in the music. Ask Tracey about the writing process and you find echoes of Dylan Thomas. It's long and tedious, he says before adding: 'Sometimes you get lucky and it writes itself and there are other times where it's uphill all the way. It's really a lonely business. You look at what you've written and have visions of the musicians chuckling up their sleeves. It's self-critical all the way. Up until the time it's actually played I'm full of self doubt.'

His suite, however, was lauded and remains a benchmark. He recorded other versions, sometimes with narration, but it's that 1965 recording that stands out: 'A rare instance of jazz accommodating an outside inspiration in a way that does justice to both,' say Morton and Cook in the Penguin guide. 'A minor masterpiece', said Derek Jewell in *The Sunday Times*.

There was no sign of *Under Milk Wood* when the newest evidence of an emerging Welsh nation opened its doors in 1999 with an official concert. But Dylan was there at the event which marked the opening of the National Assembly for Wales, in the hands of a man who'd wrestled with his Welsh roots for decades. John Cale, Garnant-born of a Welsh speaking mother and an English-speaking father, had been told at school that Thomas used English in a way that other poets used Welsh. He had imitated the Thomas style himself in lessons.

Cale had wanted to write an opera based on Thomas's life, possibly presenting a view of London and American literary lives from the point of view of an outside observer. It was evident, says Cale in his remarkable autobiography *What's Welsh for Zen?*, that at some point in that process it would mean tackling the poems – and 'the baggage' they carried. So he chose poems and started to play to them with a tape running. Eventually four were selected for Cale's *The Falklands Suite* issued on an album called *Words for the Dying in 1989*. The tracks were recorded in Russia with an orchestra; the Llandaff Cathedral Choir School (sic) add texture, particularly on 'Do Not Go Gentle'.

It's fair to say the suite had a mixed reception, but there is a charm in Cale's take on works which are so familiar to us. His 'Do Not Go Gentle' starts in a remarkably jaunty fashion (someone called it a Ronettes-type intro) but it does make you return to the work to see if you've missed something the first time round. And the second, the third – the thirty-fourth. Cale himself said he preferred the settings played on piano only rather than with full orchestra, and certainly his live piano-only performances bring out other nuances again.

And that's all artists can do when they're interpreting the works of others. They can't be saying: 'Look, I like the original, but mine's better.' They just have to put it out there and say: 'This is my take on it.'

Unless it's Daniel Jones who spent his time growing up with Dylan Thomas and then plenty of his adulthood with him too, everyone else is having a go at 'accommodating an outside inspiration'. All they've got is the words. For all he said he loved him, that's pretty much all Stravinsky had too. That's what we want from Dylan Thomas, really – words. The rest is just sound – a lot of it very beautiful; some of it neither here nor there.

Dylan Thomas: the Industry of Tragedy and the Antithetical Mask

Gary Raymond

On 8 December, 1953, almost exactly a month after the death of Dylan Thomas, Christopher Isherwood opened his diary to commit to posterity his encounters with the controversial Welsh poet. Stephen Spender had asked Isherwood to write a piece about Thomas, but Isherwood noted that: 'my memories were unsuitable for an obituary notice ... But I'd better record them here, before they get too vague.'

Isherwood, who lived in Los Angeles and had done since fleeing with Auden, England and the War in 1939, had rescued Thomas from the indifferent treatment of the English faculty at UCLA one April morning in 1950. Thomas and Isherwood had not met before, and Thomas, as was so often the case, was stuck, having been given only the number for a bus on how to reach the venue. Isherwood picked Thomas up from the 'morning desolation' of the bar at the Biltmore Hotel and drove him to the university where he was to give an afternoon reading. 'The impression he made on me was,' Isherwood wrote, 'primarily, of struggle. He seemed to be right in the midst of his life – not off on one side looking at it.'

Thomas had started the day with drink, he drank some more during a pit stop at Isherwood's house in the Valley, and then continued drinking at lunch as the guest of the English faculty. Isherwood remembers the 'bogus, oily, sanctimonious' academics at UCLA treating Thomas with 'contemptible... prissiness'. Attracted to the dangerousness in his verse, they were turned off by Thomas's performance in person, his lewdness and casual frequent deployment of the four-letter word: 'It's the attitude of the small boy,' wrote Isherwood, 'who would love (he thinks) to have the roaring tigers leap into the room out of his picture books, but who doesn't want to be afraid of them if they appear.'

Thomas got drunk before the reading, but read beautifully –

Isherwood was extremely impressed (elsewhere in his diary, many many years later, he watches Gielgud and Edith Evans recite some poems at a cocktail party in Hollywood and notes that they sounded like amateurs compared to Dylan Thomas). When the reading was over, the two of them escaped, Thomas now in excitable mood at the prospect of the entertainment Isherwood had lined up for him.

Thomas had wanted to meet a Hollywood actress – any Hollywood actress – and his idol, Charlie Chaplin, and Isherwood had used his connections for the two of them to have dinner at a restaurant with Chaplin and Shelley Winters. The meeting was either a disaster or a slapstick farce, depending on which way you look at it. Isherwood, ever the gentleman, tends to give Thomas, of whom he was clearly personally fond, the benefit of the doubt. But the facts remain that Thomas insulted Chaplin (enough for the auteur to mention it in his autobiography), before wrestling Shelley Winters to the floor over the back of her chair whilst trying to grab her breasts (Winters took it in very good humour, apparently). Later on, when the party moved on to a bar on Sunset Boulevard, and everything became even more 'muddled' with booze, Thomas tried to fight a screenwriter who had been talking to Isherwood, taking a run up to him like a cartoon bull. Thomas was, famously, as quick to dive into a brawl as he was useless in the fight. He was repelled with great ease and ran into the night. Isherwood did not see him again until a chance encounter at the Chelsea Hotel in New York almost two years later.

And so, it seems, was a somewhat typical encounter with Dylan Thomas. And as is often the case, the confluent themes of such stories involved his drinking, his inexcusable behaviour when drunk, and the genuine warmth the memoirist feels for and sees in the man. That his legend has been built just as much upon these traits as it has on his work is irrefutable; that his legend would be less had his public story been different is also quite probable. The truth is that no twentieth century writer has a posthumous reputation of such standing that is so dependent on their behavioural legend like Thomas – even writers such as Plath and Woolf, whose disintegrations have attracted an industry of comment, have their biographies subsumed by their oeuvre rather than competing with it.

But here lies the inescapable truth of Thomas – his most vital creation was not in his work, but it was in his persona. The 'Dylan' that Thomas created was what allowed him to be the poet on the page that he needed to be, it facilitated the mining of his poetical gift: a perversion of what Yeats called the 'antithetical self'.

Yeats wrote in *A Vision* of the two poles of the self, the *primary*, that which is 'reasonable and moral', and the *antithetical*, that which is our inner world of desire and imagination'. The antithetical self is familiar to the writer of fiction, it is the business of the day; but Thomas utilised an antithetical self in order to survive, not only economically, hired out as a performing monkey to the bourgeoisie, but in order that he could live in desperate loyalty to the poetic truth that he committed to paper. In more ways than one, it was his *antithetical* self, that which created his legend, that allowed his *primary* self to write.

That this creation also proved his downfall is his most powerful claim to be the patron saint of the industry of tragedy.

The prejudices, embellishments and Chinese whispers that have gone into the sculpting of Thomas's legend are a predictable offshoot of the life he first needed to live, and then became trapped by. It is extremely difficult to find any reminiscences of Thomas from his contemporaries – the people who first built his legend – that are wholly reliable; which is why Isherwood – one of the twentieth century's finest diarists; compassionate, humorous, honest – is such a good place to start when looking.

Even biographers of Thomas, such as Constantine Fitzgibbon, are unreliable in their purporting of the Thomas legend, so in thrall as they so often are to their own ego and place in the developing narrative of legend-making that they elevate their own prejudices.

In Fitzgibbon's case, an aggressive anti-communist, it is clearly difficult for him to hide his disdain of figures such as the 'King of Bohemia' and sometime affiliate of the anarchist movement, Augustus John, whose recorded reminiscences of his long-time friendship with Thomas (it was John who introduced Dylan to Caitlin) may not always be flattering, but they are at least disinterested in the moulding of any legend at all. (Check out passing jibes from Fitzgibbon when writing about John '... who, in those pre-war years, promised to become a great painter. That he failed fully to keep this promise was due above all to his extravagant tastes...'). Fitzgibbon takes similar snide shots at anybody else who did not find Thomas as entertaining as they were supposed to.

Fitzgibbon instead decides to align Thomas with the oddly correlative figure of Theodore Roethke, the big, womanising, alcoholic, German American poet, who likewise died prematurely (a heart attack at fifty-five) due to his excessive lifestyle. (That Roethke, often referred to as the greatest American poet of the twentieth century, has not been subjected to the same canonisation as Thomas perhaps lies in America's lack of need for *yet another* hell-raising writer).

Roethke himself remembered Thomas, whom he knew and drank with for a relatively brief period in Los Angeles, as 'one of the great ones, there can be no doubt about that. And he drank his own blood, ate his own marrow, to get at some of that material.' They are powerful, passionate words, from one great poet to another, and in a small way, they elevate the writer of them as much as they do the eulogised. Nobody doubts the kineticism of the well from which Thomas drew his poetics, but here at work are the subtle cogs of myth-making. To champion greatness can create an exalted, esoteric pool in which recognised and recogniser swim together.

This is the starkest evidence that Thomas no longer belongs to himself, he belongs to that industry of tragedy; and it is an important part of the artists' code, the thing that makes the world go round. (Thomas would no doubt be over the moon to see how he was adopted by the literati in his death as a totemic figure of artistic sacrifice). Figures like Thomas are integral to the standing of the artistic community – the danger, the mysticism, the otherness. That so many people recognised the potential of Thomas the Legend and that so many chipped in to consolidate it after his death, is proof enough that the lucrative offshoot was cultural as well as fiscal. In poetry particularly, from Byron to Wordsworth through Clare and Swinburne to Pound and Plath, reputation for eccentricity and danger is priceless when viewed as sincere. Mix that with an early death, and a poetic destiny that somehow matches a writer of verse with an otherworldly essence, and you have an irresistible legend, one that reaches way beyond the readers of poems.

When writing the lives of Thomas's friends and acquaintances, literary biographers have likewise been quick to use just the two dimensions of Thomas to draw something out of their own subject, often contributing to the skewed public character of Thomas himself. Arthur Koestler's biographer Michael Scammell noted the attraction between the two fabled drinking partners as a 'shared disregard for bourgeois politesse.' Their eyes met across a crowded room and mischievousness sparked.

But Koestler was a brawler, a reactionary, a former vagabond who used to argue down Sartre and de Beauvoir into states of turpitude; Koestler was an intellectual giant whose oxygen was tearing strips off people in public drunken debate. Thomas was a very different creature indeed, although in his own way just as complex. To bind the two with their puerile scoffing adds colour to Koestler, but adds more monochrome to the picture of Thomas as parochial clown. Whereas Koestler was once described as a 'noble goblin', Thomas is most often referred to in later years as 'puffy'. There is always a condescending tone, even from his acolytes, in many accounts of encounters with the bumpkin Thomas; perhaps if he had ever learned to land a punch, like Koestler or the fearsome Roy Campbell often did (the three of them making Soho their drunken playground during the War), Thomas may have been written about quite differently.

But it was the certainly more placid and decidedly more circumspect Stephen Spender who Thomas first encountered in London. Spender, in his *Paris Review* interview of 1980, which is bulbous with delicious anecdotes about his encounters with the likes of Yeats, Hemingway and Woolf, recounts his first meeting with Thomas. They have lunch in a pub in Soho, Thomas, Spender, and a friend of Spender's, invited along to ensure awkward silences were broken up. And the friend is needed, as Thomas is nervous and pale and largely silent. This is the Thomas before he was the hired entertainment *de rigueur* of the socialite scene.

Spender pulls back to an overview of his relationship with Thomas; he tells how many years later Thomas wrote him a very warm letter thanking him for the hospitality Spender had shown him when he first came to London. And then Spender says: 'He certainly said extremely mean things about me behind my back, of that I'm quite sure. I don't hold that against him. It was just his style. We all enjoy doing things like that.'

Here we see the melee into which Thomas was flung in the days and months and years following that initial quiet lunch with Spender on arrival. The biting gladiatorial throng, so well embodied in the legends of the Bloomsbury set, was in full flow, and Thomas was going to have to step up if he was to stand out. He certainly did that, as the story goes, by becoming more and more rambunctious and unpredictable, more shocking, the bumpkin Byron.

But was Thomas malleable to a scene, rather than stuck in one, or was he just ignorant and naïve? How calculated was this mask? His personal loyalties certainly seemed reactive, and not formed with one eye on the shifting winds. For example, Roy Campbell was *persona non grata* with the Bloomsbury set after his *Georgiad* lampooned the main figures, (that he was also prone to brawling, jumping on stage and swiping at Stephen Spender at a poetry recital, and throwing Jacob Epstein around a bar, probably didn't help either). But when Generals Franco and Mola came up from Morocco in 1936 and sparked the Spanish Revolution, Campbell, a staunch Catholic, came out on the side of the brutal and murderous Nationalists, contrary to most intellectual opinion in England and the time.

Thomas, it seemed, ignored both the school yard spats and the rather more serious political standpoints of Campbell, and continued friendships on both sides of the divide. Campbell, many years later, wrote about his appreciation for Thomas's lack of politicking in these matters; but one must consider Thomas' loyalty to Campbell as perhaps being somewhat lacking in principle rather than smacking of it. Perhaps it was the loyalty of a friend, to stand by a supporter of fascism; or perhaps when John Malcolm Brinnin commented that Thomas's socialism seemed a pose, and half-hearted, something simply expected from his Welshness, he was hitting the nail firmly on the head. Thomas, in the end, was ignorant of the politics, and he just sided with his drinking buddy.

Of course, Campbell and Thomas (and Koestler) had more in common than just alcoholism: they were always broke. Money, or lack of, is another heavy colour to the Thomas story, and was the strongest compulsion in the creation of his public character.

It is worth noting here something of the character of the people who created the legend of Dylan Thomas. They were often those unfurled from the rarefied cloisters of Oxbridge, which further accounts for the condescending tone to which Thomas the person is often subjected in print. It also accounts for the tincture of vulgarity in Thomas's portrait which goes beyond reaction to his brazen lewdness. Someone like Stephen Spender, who although hardly English aristocracy, came from a more entitled world than Cwmdonkin Drive, commented on how Thomas was 'rather obsessed by money' – ever the viewpoint of one who had rarely needed for it when looking to someone who was perpetually struggling to feed his wife and children.

Thomas worked hard to make ends meet, to put food on the table. Perhaps his refusal to do any work to which he was not physically or intellectually suited would be lambasted in certain circles (especially in today's economically myopic censorious political climate), but in hindsight it is difficult to criticise his simple wish to feed his children using his talents, especially as they were so widely appreciated.

Thomas's predicament, and his stresses, is displayed in painful poignancy in a brief correspondence with Graham Greene in 1947. Greene is an influential figure in the British film industry at this point, and Thomas tries to impress upon him an old script he had written about Edinburgh grave robbers Burke and Hare. The note soon degenerates into a begging letter. Michael Redgrave has shown interest in playing in it, he writes, before a ham-handed segue into a plea regarding his infant son's medical bills and the writs that keep falling on the welcome mat. It is painful to read. Thomas wrote an uncountable number of such letters throughout his life.

What we see here is the reality of Thomas's existence, and the strain it put on him. He was certainly not alone in his penury as an artist, but there was money to be made, one way or the other, in poetry during the Thirties and Forties, it's just Thomas could not find a way into the middle-class hold. But he had something he had been inadvertently developing that he knew he could mine: his public personality, the 'antithetical mask'.

And so as the legend began, it is quite remarkable how quickly Thomas grew to look at his new role, and the demands of it, as a curse.

Novelist and poet Rayner Heppenstall recalls one evening drinking with Thomas (Thomas downing some local Cornish moonshine), when Thomas breathlessly held court for quite some time before stopping and declaring rather sadly, 'Somebody's boring me. And I think it's me.'

Already, the man trapped.

After his death, this very real need was turned into a romantic tragedy by Thomas's contemporaries. Karl Shapiro wrote in 1955: 'Thomas was the first modern romantic poet you could put your finger on, the first whose journeys and itineraries became part of his own mythology, the first who offered himself up as a public sacrifice.'

A sacrifice?! To the gods of poetry, no less!? A cursory reading of Thomas's own letters shows clearly a man just trying to feed his kids. But Shapiro subscribes to an idea integral to Thomas's legend when he goes on to write: 'How much did Thomas subscribe to official Symbolism? ... How much did he love death as his major symbol? As much as any poet I know in the English language. These factions have a claim on Thomas which we cannot fully contradict.'

But Thomas was not obsessed with symbols of death because in some ethereal poetic bubble he could see his destiny in his posthumous legend. The compulsions of Thomas were far more earthbound, far more serious than intellectual legacy or celestial aesthetic vocation. It can be put quite simply: it was Thomas's refusal to dig ditches for a living, because of his unquestioning belief in loyalty to his gifts, that meant he had to become a performing monkey for socialites and literati in order to feed his children; his alcoholism gained legitimacy not only as Dutch courage, but as part of his act, and his alcoholism gave him nothing in the tank when pneumonia came, and the pneumonia killed him.

And it was in death that Thomas was moved effortlessly, without his say so, from performing monkey to patron saint of the ever-vibrant industry of tragedy. For many years after, publications traded on the memories of and encounters with the Hell Raiser and Genius Dylan Thomas. That Isherwood never published his reflection on Thomas (until the publication of *Diaries*, that is, in 1996), adds much weight to the accuracy of it. Many other writers, even those who had always been so opposed to Thomas and his work, were happy to add to his legend.

Kingsley Amis, who never quite came to terms with either Thomas's work or his fame, on news of Thomas's death wrote to Philip Larkin, 'I don't grieve for him as a voice for ever silenced, in fact that part of it is pretty much all right with me.'

That Amis thought this is important because it differs in tone from what he published on the subject, for *The Spectator* in 1957.

There are two accounts from Amis, a private one and a published one, of his meeting with Dylan Thomas at one of Thomas's readings at Swansea University when Amis was just twenty-eight. *The Spectator* account is softer, much more sympathetic, although the bare bones of the story remain the same. The Thomas of *The Spectator* article certainly appears to be a trapped public figure. We are introduced to the Thomas of the tragic myth, he is beleaguered and battered, drunk and isolated, pecked at by a hanger on, Thomas too 'good natured' to ever turn someone away. Amis concludes that, contrary to his own previously held conception, that Thomas' 'attitude was the product of nothing more self-aware or self-regarding than shyness.' Whether true or not, Amis is contributing to the legend of Thomas, as one who moved about us with the black cloud of his own tragic, poetic destiny overhead, a destiny now fulfilled.

In private, Amis was cutting of Thomas's 'performance', it being filled with 'ragged epigrams topped up with some impressionistic stuff about America ... [and] a backlash of dutiful impropriety. And the poems he spoke out with his mouth: ooh corks! He fucked up two of Auden's things from *Another Time* ... In the pub afterwards, the more intelligent students sneered at him gently, and he perceived this.' Amis's prejudice against Thomas's work informs his rhetoric, just as his awareness of the industry of tragedy informs the tone of his piece for *The Spectator*; and so the significance of the pieces lies not in the truth of Thomas' character, but in the rigidity of the construction of his legend. Of his work Amis was as damning as he had always been. He once wrote to Larkin, 'I just wish he'd GROW UP', and made overt reference to what he saw as Thomas dressing up a trite idea in language designed to prevent people from seeing how trite it is. Whether Amis is right or not about the poem in question (he does not name it in the letter) is perhaps beside the point; what Amis alludes to here is the art of showmanship, of showbiz, of populism.

What Amis claims is that Thomas is not what he is held up to be. Perhaps Amis, in his staunch opposition, saw a central truth to Thomas, even if not for the right reasons. Is it possible that Thomas's popularity then and now is due in part to the public being wooed by the idea of complexity, the garb of intellectualism, when in fact there is little profound going on? Add to that the fact that Thomas's legend is attractive in ways that his work is not – the industry of tragedy is and always has been more alluring than the business of poetry, even when the two are bedfellows.

Significantly, what Kingsley Amis identifies as showmanship he does not associate with charlatanism. He explicitly rejects the idea, in private, that Thomas is a fake, but rather, 'a second rate GK Chesterton … you know: frothing at the mouth with piss'.

It is no wonder that from all of this a simple, billboard-friendly, and utterly vaporous, idea of the man has emerged; it is Thomas's own creation after all, one that became so potent it continues to outlive his *primary* self.

Truth, Lies and Poetry

D.J. Britton

> Let it be known
> That nothing lives but lies,
> Love-lies and God-lies and lies to please...

I came across these lines from one of Dylan Thomas's lesser-known poems[1] while collecting material for my play *Chelsea Dreaming*[2] a few years ago. The significance of lies in human discourse had been rattling around in my head for years, and Thomas's unequivocal lines had me frowning into a philosophical abyss. Did he really believe that life was a lie? Or was this just the bombastic generalisation of an ambitious poet in his formative years?

Chelsea Dreaming imagines a conversation between Thomas and the shabbily glorious Chelsea Hotel, where he spent his last conscious days in New York. Dylan tries to impress the Hotel by exaggerating his own bad behaviour. It is a conversation he cannot win. Whatever Dylan's outrageous claims, the notorious Chelsea Hotel has seen more, bigger, worse. A building which has hosted everything from Sarah Bernhardt demanding that her bed be replaced by a coffin (so that she could experience what it felt like to wake up dead) to Sid Vicious and Nancy Spungeon's drug-fuelled fatal final days together, is certainly not impressed by Thomas's eighteen straight whiskies.

Using choral chant and enhanced by Paula Gardiner's powerful jazz score, *Chelsea Dreaming* sets the feebleness of Thomas's lying lifestyle against the lyric genius of his poetry. The Hotel has no time for the former but recognises the importance of the latter.

Dylan Thomas was a magnificent liar, much to the entertainment of those in the glow of his momentary friendship and often to the intense pain and humiliation of those outside of the circle. Dylan could use his gift of language to cajole and bully and crush, to chisel and wheedle and extort. Not for nothing did his enemies in the pubs of London's Fitzrovia call him the Ugly Suckling. A facility with words is no guarantee that we will use them honestly or kindly.

Yet here is the conundrum. At its best, Dylan's writing lives not on lies; it touches great universal truths. Rereading 'Do Not Go Gentle' after my own father's death I felt my legs taken from under me. How could another man, in another place at another time, capture the grief, anger, fear and love that I alone was experiencing?

In one of my earliest stage works *Cargo,* the heroine is Sarka, an activist in the 1968 Czech rebellion. She tells her lover Phil, a morally ambiguous and linguistically sloppy Australian protest singer: 'I have lived twenty-five years surrounded by words: television, radio, newspapers, books. Many, many words, most of them ... inaccurate.'

Sarka explains that she and her friends have learnt to believe information only from people they know personally and trust: 'We put our lives in each other's hands and to do this we must respect what we say, the words we use to each other.' In Sarka's world, lies are what the enemy speaks. You do not lie to your friends.

Brought up in a world of secret police, propaganda and lies, Sarka is a truth fundamentalist. She sees blunt honesty as her nation's only path to salvation. She is also, as Phil discovers, impossibly difficult to live with. As Paul Simon puts it:

> Honesty...
> It's such a waste of energy
> You don't have to lie to me
> Just give me some tenderness
> Beneath your honesty.[3]

In this age of constant surveillance, to be caught in a lie or tainted by hypocrisy is to be accused of an unforgiveable crime. President Clinton was turfed out of office not because he was a lecherous older man who ought to have known better, but because he had 'lied to the American People'. Over the past decade political/media speak in the UK has followed that transatlantic trend. Politicians now talk about the 'British People' as if those who live in Wales, Scotland, Northern Ireland

and England are some sort of singular shell-shocked entity, rather than millions of disparate people who, through friendship, love, family and the biff-and-bang of everyday life, can decide for themselves whom they trust (and to what extent) and whose lies they might be inclined to tolerate a little. That's how ordinary people get by.

Hypocrisy may be unpopular but must it always be a cause for hate? I would rather people aspire to decent actions, and fail to live up to the standards they have set themselves, than to start out by embracing poor behaviour and honestly living down to those miserable standards. If we live in constant fear of being trapped in hypocrisy we will live, quite simply, in constant fear of aspiration.

In *Under Milk Wood*, Thomas writes of The Inspectors of Cruelty, who are, in fact The Defenders of Truth who frown down upon the lying Butcher Beynon with his grisly fibbing stories of man-chops and corgi meat. Today's Defenders of Truth are not the Chapel tut-tutters whom Thomas undoubtedly had in mind, but media organisations who point an accusatory finger while themselves trading, variously, in soft porn, celebrity PR, fear, loathing and shallow Westminster gossip. Revelation through public exposure is an important tool which responsible journalists have used effectively and for the common good on notable occasions in recent years. It should be defended. But the importance of this investigative role is diminished when unscrupulous media operators become convinced of their right to an unfettered search for the private truths which lurk in our little lives. Phone hacking was not an aberration. It was the by-product of a culture addicted to instant information.

Anton Pavlovich Chekhov, the guiding star of modern playwrights, knew about truth and lies, and the part they play in our lives.

In his early career as a doctor, Chekhov observed tendencies in human behaviour which dramatists even now too often forget. He noted that people rarely say what they are thinking; that a man who comes to the surgery suffering from a headache may, in fact, be suffering from a guilty conscience or an unfaithful wife.

He saw that it was not so much *what* was said that was important but *why* it was being said; whose benefit it was for, what the intended effect might be. Above all Chekhov knew that what was withheld was just as important as what was said.

His characters are not for the most part deliberate liars, but they are the creators and purveyors of endless untruths. They lie to themselves about the realities of life. They lie to themselves about what they are feeling. And, for a multiplicity of reasons, they withhold the truth from others. In *Three Sisters*, the schoolteacher Kulygin, full of false bonhomie, chants, mantra-like: 'Masha loves me, my wife loves me ... I am content, I am content.' Who is he kidding? Not those around him, not the audience, probably not even himself. But the lie gives him hope. In a magnificent unspoken moment of drama, we realise that Kulygin has known all along that Masha has been having an affair with Vershinin (himself a man who avoids his own problems through romantic escapism). Now that the affair is over Kulygin will care for Masha whether she wants it or not. Kindly, yes. Boringly, probably. For that is their unspoken truth.

> Let it be known
> That nothing lives but lies,
> Life lies and God-lies and lies to please...

In his humane genius, Chekhov understands that the lies of his characters are merely superficial, sad and comic. They are simply the means by which the people survive. Beneath these lies are deeper truths which persist even though they may not be spoken. His characters are by and large hypocrites, yet Anton Pavlovich still loves them, and so do I. Pretty little Irina sits in bed all morning enthusing romantically about the joys of work. When, eventually, she does get a job she soon learns to speak scornfully of the banality of mundane employment. And despite her yearning for real passion, she agrees to marry Tusenbach, a good man but someone she does not love.

Before Tusenbach heads off to certain death in a secret duel, he conceals the truth and asks Irina, instead, to have the servants make some coffee ready for his return. That's his exit – a feeble, brave, lie. And in that moment, Irina – ignorant of his fate – decides to be dogmatic about the truth and tells him she cannot love him. In the audience, I am almost shouting from the stalls to her, begging her to be a hypocrite. The poor man's doomed, for goodness sake. Tell him you love him. Lie! Perhaps the greatest mystery of the entire play concerns the self-loathing ageing doctor, Chebutykin. The one constant in his cynical empty life is his distant love for Irina's long-dead mother. Is it merely the echo of the mother which maintains his endless affection for the daughter? Or is it the never-spoken possibility that he is, in fact, Irina's father? Either way, it is the unsaid which gives Chebutykin his humanity.

So many lies, yet so many deeper truths.

Where then, should veracity sit in the creative mind of the modern writer? Within a couple of years of Dylan's death, Britain's traditionally muted approach to self-examination was being assailed by Angry Young Men, writers determined to pick at the sores of post war society. In dramatic writing, John Osborne's *Look Back in Anger* muscled onto stage at the London Royal Court, beginning a new movement in which direct societal examination would become the primary focus of British theatre, plays emerging from every newly perceived unfairness, every dark obsession. There is a journalistic zeal associated with this still dominant movement, an urge to reveal the Great Lie which lurks behind our twenty-first-century agony. Encouraged by critics, stage writers have in recent years taken further steps down this path, turning first towards documentary drama and then to Verbatim Theatre, in which the stage dialogue is edited from literal reportage – for example from words actually spoken in a significant court case.

Is this direct and functional approach to the search for truth the most useful form of theatre? Sometimes, perhaps. One thing is clear: journalistic dramas tend to attract journalistic attention because journalists understand them and the issues they address. The same goes for the contemporary factually-grounded novel. Certainly I would not want a return to the drawing room plays of the pre-war period. But an artistic form which has the metaphoric power to illuminate huge universal issues through moments of focussed humanity surely has a greater potential. Imaginative writing, be it theatrical, literary or poetic, can whisper or sing or calmly recount so much more than the indignant shout of reportage, especially when we are already subject to the angry cacophony of twenty-four-hour news-shout.

The most skilled modern playwrights do manage to merge theatre's timeless universality with contemporary comment. In *Bloody Poetry*[4], for example, Howard Brenton gives a fierce and funny critique of 1980s celebrity culture and its grovelling gutter press through a narrative built around the poets Byron and Shelley and their lovers Mary Shelley and Claire Claremont. Dylan Thomas may have fancied himself as the Rimbaud of Cwmdonkin Drive, but on rereading *Bloody Poetry* it is Byron one can imagine sharing a Chelsea Hotel rampage with Dylan, the first rock star of poetry making mischief with his 1950s counterpart. One wonderful exchange in *Bloody Poetry* has Polidori, the doctor/journalist sent to spy on the ménage, suffering from the savage cruelty of Byron's wit. When he complains Lord Byron replies: 'My abuse is a gift. It will enrich your life.'

That might have been Dylan in one of his Fitzrovia watering holes.

Sir Philip Sidney, the sixteenth-century poet, soldier and courtier, gave much thought to honour, truth and the place of the writer in the wider world. Philip was the son of Sir Henry Sidney, Lord Protector of Wales, a man whose very title was a lie; his job was not to protect Wales but to oversee it – from the safety of English Shrewsbury. He was, in fact, protecting the English from the fear of Welsh insurrection. Henry also became Lord Protector of Ireland, a title hilariously inappropriate. Political double-speak was not, after all, invented by George Orwell; to Dylan's '*Let it be known*' we might well add the line '*...and lies to hide*'. Politicians have been at it a very long time.

Philip Sidney wrote (some would say co-wrote with his sister Mary) the *Arcadia*[5], for 200 years Britain's most-read work of fiction. The fact that he was a fine poet, did not stop him from considering carefully the pitfalls and pratfalls of poetry. In his *Defence of Poesy*, Sidney considers the poet who, walking at night with his eyes turned upwards in wonder to the stars, falls into a ditch. It is a point well made. But I do wonder if today we sometimes spend so much time poking around in the ditch looking for lies that we forget to look upwards to the stars in search of bigger truths.

Dylan Thomas had an instinctive insight into the truths of the human condition. He had the ability to look both outward at the world and inward to his own soul. This, linked to an astounding lyrical gift, makes him a timeless singer of humanity's song, a great poet. Why then, was he such a liar in his own life? And why the contention that 'nothing lives but lies'. Did he really believe it?

Probably there are sound psychological reasons for Dylan's behaviour. Or perhaps, through literary analysis, the backward tracing from poetry to the poet, we may find causal motivation. However, I suspect it may be more useful to consider a less intellectual aspect of Dylan's life.

Writers live in a constant tension between the private pleasure of placing their thoughts on the page, and the desperate hope that this privacy will become public when someone wants to read it. Unless they choose to publish anonymously (and few do) even the most reticent writer must overcome his or her shyness in order to share their thoughts and feelings. For some this may emerge as a need to please. For others it may manifest itself as a need to shock. Either way, it can become a trap.

Dylan sought attention. From his early days performing at Swansea's Little Theatre to his final public reading in the USA, he wanted to be at the centre of things.

As one early exchange in *Chelsea Dreaming* has it:

CHELSEA   *Room service.*
DYLAN   *I need an audience.*
CHELSEA   *The death hours of a New York November morning*
           and he wants an audience.
DYLAN   *NEED! I need an audience…*
           And a bottle of whisky from the White Horse.

As every bar-room bull-shitter knows, invention, exaggeration and sensationalism are the meat and drink to the attention-seeker. But the struggle between the outward attractions of public notoriety and the inward journey which bonds deep thought with artistic expression can be darkly destructive. The interwoven path of private insight and public presentation offers little high ground and many muddy puddles. In some senses Dylan had it lucky. His success came before the huge publicity-marketing machine of the late twentieth century stepped up the process of turning artists into commodities. But he did indeed need an audience and unlike more circumspect personalities, he let it take him over.

In his comic and sharply observational *Cautionary Verses*[6] Hilaire Belloc (who coincidentally died in the same year as Thomas) writes about one Edwardian young lady who needed an audience more than most:

> Matilda told such Dreadful Lies,
> It made one Gasp and Stretch one's Eyes;
> Her Aunt, who from her Earliest Youth,
> Had kept a Strict Regard for Truth,
> Attempted to Believe Matilda:
> The effort very nearly killed her,
> And would have done so, had not she
> Discovered this Infirmity.

In a moment of boredom while her Aunt is out at the theatre, Matilda makes what we would now call a hoax call to the fire brigade. Much attention, much consternation from her Aunt. When her Aunt goes out again, and Matilda repeats the prank, no-one believes her...

> For every time She shouted 'Fire!'
> They only answered 'Little Liar!'
> And therefore when her Aunt returned,
> Matilda, and the House, were burned.

Like Matilda, the real-life Dylan lied when it suited him, to feed his need for attention – even though his poetic vision was capable of touching on great truths. And as with Matilda, the lies burned him up.

In *Chelsea Dreaming*, the bragging, the lies, don't cut it with the Hotel. What does impress is Dylan's poetic truth. Is it possible to have one without the other? I'm still uncertain, but like the Chelsea, I prefer to remember him for his transcendental vision rather than for his earthbound banality.

Does nothing live but lies? I don't think so. And nor, I suspect, did Dylan. *Let it be known...* was not, after all published in his lifetime (although neither did Dylan destroy it; he kept it in his notebook). On the other hand, the lines are impressive. They do have a swagger. Not unlike the start of a very good – and not necessarily very truthful – pub yarn, told by a bit of a show-off.

1: Dylan Thomas, *The Notebook Poems 1930-1934*, edited by Ralph Maud (Dent, 1989).

2: D.J. Britton, *Chelsea Dreaming* (BBC Audiobooks, 2004).

3: Paul Simon, 'Tenderness' from *There Goes Rhymin' Simon*, Columbia Records, 1973.

4: Howard Brenton, 'Bloody Poetry' in *Plays: Two* (Methuen, 1989).

5: Sir Philip Sidney, *The Countess of Pembroke's Arcadia* (Penguin Classics, 1977).

6: H.Belloc, *Cautionary Tales for Children* (Duckworth, 1940).

Dylan & Me

Guy Masterson

I properly came to Dylan Thomas relatively late – at the age of nineteen to be precise, in a sun blessed library over a garage in Celigny, near Geneva in Switzerland. The words, 'Listen to this...' were followed by 'To begin at the beginning...' and the rest of the opening monologue from *Under Milk Wood*. I say 'properly' because, of course, it was not the first time I'd heard those words. I could recall hearing them several times over the years; at home from a scratchy LP that my mam occasionally put on, on the radio and, very occasionally on the TV... though I never paid them much heed and certainly didn't listen for too much longer. But this time, a captive audience, I could do little but put down the book I was reading and listen... and listen and look... For the first time, I could 'see' the shapes and characters emerging from those words. My imagination was being sparked. My mind's eye was replacing my real vision with that of the Welsh wizard and I was becoming entranced.

At the time, I was attending Cardiff University studying Biochemistry and Chemistry yet, even surrounded by fellow countrymen, I was still blissfully ignorant of our finest literary genius. I had heard of him, of course, but knowing the title of his masterpiece was the sum of my knowledge... until that morning in Celigny.

I should add that I was in Celigny at the request of my great uncle who had purchased a dragon-red Mini-Cooper S and had asked me to drive it to his home in Switzerland. He was unable to do so himself as he had recently undergone a life-saving spinal operation and his neck was still in a brace. He'd not yet recovered enough upper-body strength to control this most wayward of minxes. Indeed this particular model, a mint '67, one of the last to be made, possessed a peculiar wobble, evident only at the exact speed of 55mph, upon which it would veer sharply to the right only to be over-corrected to the left and thence to the right etc... and said wobble could only be overcome by sharp braking or, as I soon mastered, accelerating to 65mph, which it could achieve with remarkable swiftness, after which, it would zoom along, as smooth as silk. Thankfully, said wobble did not manifest while slowing down through 55mph, so the danger was only present when speeding up. This was, of course, the best excuse to travel at extremely high speeds in a very small car – which only heightened the thrill.

So, being only 19 and something of 'a lad', driving my uncle's Cooper-S was a veritable dream-come-true. Whizzing around the local streets making lots of noise, I definitely attracted attention, some of it female, and loved it. The tricky part would be driving her to Switzerland. Not only would it be the longest drive I had attempted, most of it would be on the wrong side of the road... a new experience, and one my mam was keen to prevent. But, after much remonstration with her uncle-cum-brother – for that is what he really was to her – it was agreed that I could drive the Cooper-S to Celigny as long as he accompanied me – as he, very kindly, offered to do.

To clarify; this great uncle of mine, though technically my mam's normal uncle through being my Grandma's younger brother, was only two when their mam died, so Grandma, recently married and twenty years older, took him in and brought him up as my mam's brother... And Mam never called him 'uncle'... She only referred to him by his first name of 'Rich', and they treated each other as siblings... To me and to all my siblings and cousins, he was just 'Uncle Rich', and this is how I still refer to him, even thrity years after his passing.

Anyhow, at daybreak on that blissful 14 July morning, we set off for Paris via Dover en route to Switzerland, on our first road trip. After an eventful first leg (on which I will not elucidate further for this is not the subject of this essay) we arrived in Paris during the late afternoon rush – which, even on Bastille Day is something to be reckoned with. My first ever night on the continent was met with street parties and fireworks. Noisy, exciting and, I suppose, fitting...

After two weeks staying with Uncle Rich's rich friends just off the Trois D'Etoille, I finally drove the rest of the trip to Celigny by myself. Well, to be truthful, I was not entirely by myself. I drove the second leg without him. I was accompanied by a young lass, a college friend, to whom I had lost my heart, and whom Uncle Rich had insisted upon inviting to keep me company. He was secretly hoping that my unrequited love would become requited during the trip and had 'managed' the sleeping arrangements to enhance my chances. However, I can attest today that no such luck found its way to me, even though my honour was sorely tempted. So, this part of his plan entailed sending me on my way without him, but with her. Sadly, it didn't work.

He and I met up again at his home in Celigny, appropriately named 'Pays de Galles'. Having arrived at three in the morning – a ridiculous attempt at saving the money he'd given us for a hotel room en route. He woke me at dawn with a bemused rap on the window and a cup of tea in hand.

We stayed there for a few weeks during which he would get up at an obscene hour in the morning to go to his library above the garage and read. Light sleeper as I am, I would get up too, grab a cuppa, and go with him, and there we would sit... reading, in the cool morning sunshine, occasionally talking. I would do most of the listening for he was fascinating. And he would often read to me excerpts from poems or books or Shakespeare. And on that one memorable occasion, he recited the opening monologue from *Under Milk Wood*...

Looking back, I know now that a seed was planted. I fell in love that day, with the enchanting words of Dylan Thomas and the bewitching voice of my great uncle. It was a voice I had heard many times before; at home of course, but also on the TV, in the cinema, on the radio and the record player, but here, in the sun-kissed library in Celigny, I had that voice all to myself. It was achingly personal and it was being given to me like a special gift, and in that voice were the words of another great Welshman. Of course I was enchanted. How could I not be? That voice belonged to Richard Burton.

Uncle Rich died at home in Celigny on 5 August, 1984, just over three years later. I was then living in Hollywood and dating an actress. I was devastated. For days, news of his death was knocking the Los Angeles Olympics off the front page. I knew he was a 'superstar' but had no real concept of what that meant.

Up to that moment, I done what he'd encouraged me to: 'Be a good boy and finish your degree!' But I knew that genetic research was not what I was cut out for and, in truth, living in Hollywood and the lure of Hollywood were merging. I was becoming interested in acting... It was my girlfriend that watered the seed. She insisted that I join her in an acting class which, after some resistance, I did, having taught myself a monologue from *Hamlet* as an audition piece.

One of my prized possessions, much more so since he'd died, was a box set of Uncle Rich's 1964 Broadway *Hamlet* directed by John Gielgud, which I'd listened to religiously. So, it was the easiest thing to learn one of Hamlet's soliloquies with Uncle Richard's voice swimming about in my head. Not quite so easy to recite it for entry to my first acting class, but I did so, with all the Burtonisms I could muster. The response from the class was muted, but encouraging. Could I perhaps do it again, but using my own voice this time? I did so and the response was much more positive. I was invited by the tutor and the group to join the class. I was going to study to become an actor! I was going to follow in my Great Uncle's footsteps. That was the plan.

Of course, it isn't as easy as that. Saying you're an actor is one thing. Being an actor is another. Becoming a globally renowned superstar actor is off the scale. But aspiring to be all three was okay though.

One of the first things they did when I joined the acting class was to put a book in my hand called *Voice and the Actor* by the eminent British vocal coach, Cecily Berry. They asked me to turn to page thirty-five and to read the passage on that page as clearly and as quickly as I could. It was a vocal warm up exercise designed to get the lips and teeth and tongue going: 'And the shrill girls giggle and muster around him and squeal as they clutch and thrash...' a passage from the heart of *Under Milk Wood* when little Dickie gets tormented by the girls and runs home in tears ('through the weeping end of the world') and I recited this passage with gusto, relishing all the vowels and consonants as they tumbled off my tongue in my native south Welsh dialect tempered with a London twang. The marriage of Dylan's words and my voice, my heart and my spirit unleashed a force in me that I will never forget. Their natural, instinctive rhythm, their cadence, their richness, the sheer joy of uttering those words was, for want of a better one, intoxicating. I had, at last, found something that really made my soul vibrate, but even more importantly was that, as much as I wanted to be like Richard Burton, I needed no vocal aid from him to make those particular words sing. I had at last found a voice of my own.

It could be said that Richard Burton was largely responsible for the success of *Under Milk Wood*. Don't get me wrong, it is very likely to have found its way to the pinnacle of our national works of literary genius... eventually, but because Richard Burton, personal friend of Dylan, London stage and two time Oscar-nominated Hollywood star, had taken on the role of First Voice, its inaugural broadcast found a much greater and perhaps more popular audience than it might have done, even with Dylan himself in the role as originally planned. Sadly, the posthumous acclaim which it received was too late to help the tragically broke Thomas but it did, however, stimulate a wider interest in Dylan's work and his legacy has never looked back.

Cut to 1993; while I was playing Robert Lindsay's West End production of *Cyrano de Bergerac* and searching in vain for a new agent, I decided to take a more personal control of my career. Having been inspired by Steven Berkoff's solo work, where, on an empty stage with no props but great words, he could command his audience for ninety spellbinding minutes, I chose to attempt to perform *Under Milk Wood* – in its entirety – in the same way using nothing but the words. I gave myself only two rules. I would do it word for word, comma for comma, unexpurgated – no edits – and, I would do it without props. The idea being that I would learn all the words and try to allow them to work their magic on my imagination, from which I would perform. I wanted it to be pure.

This may seem strange, but from the outset, I never found the prospect daunting. I already knew about the relentless graft in making a solo play with my first one-man show a couple of years earlier, *The Boy's Own Story* by Peter Flannery. With this I knew I could survive on my own in front of an audience. And I also knew that four hours a day for two months learning the script was just par for the course. It had to be done. There was no other way to do it. So, I set about methodically repeating the magical words of Dylan's masterpiece over and over, time after time until they started tumbling out of my mouth, all in the right order, without my having to think about it, until I could recite the entire work from beginning to end without even having to check the script. Graft. Pure. Two months of. No other word for it.

Of course, learning it was one thing. 'Putting it on its feet' (as we call it), was a different thing entirely. How would I delineate between Dylan's myriad characters without costumes or props? And how would the audience know who was talking? How would they follow the narrative? Well, the truth is, I had absolutely no idea. I had no preconceptions about how to do it or how it would be received. It was an experiment, pure and simple.

They say that 'the proof of the pudding is in the eating'. In learning and reciting the words over and over, my imagination took control. Images of the characters as they spoke would pop into my mind. I could see uncles and aunties, cousins and multiple lesser relatives appear before my eyes, and I would mimic their mannerisms, copy their cadences, fake their physicality. I would people Dylan's play with characters from my imagination stimulated by his words. I would, in effect, animate Llarregub.

Most importantly, I would not glue on mannerisms or characteristics that might look or feel right. I would 'permit' my imagination and 'allow' my body and voice to interpret it. More 'being' than 'doing'. I guess what I am trying to say is that I wouldn't try to act out *Under Milk Wood,* I'd try to become *Under Milk Wood*. But I had no idea if it would work.

The first time I put it in front of an audience, three months later, was at the Little Theatre on the Isle of Sheppey, which is about as remote as I could wish for. If I was to make an idiot of myself it would be in front of people I would very likely never see again. That was the plan, anyway. If I remember rightly, there were four people there. An auspicious start you might say! But somehow my solo version of *Under Milk Wood* had flown after all. It was September 1993.

I approached the Traverse Theatre in Edinburgh – known to be open to experimental small scale works – on a tip off that they had an empty week in February 1994 and asked if they would be interested in putting on a one-man version of '*Under Milk Wood*, uncut, unexpurgated?' Intrigued but not convinced: 'a bit ambitious?' and 'who the hell are you?' But, about a week or so later, I got a call from someone in their marketing team.

'Is it true that you are Richard Burton's nephew?'

'Yes,' I admitted, 'he happened to be my Uncle', and that was it. They made me an offer to premiere the show in Edinburgh that February. I could do it for no upfront fee and no expenses, but a healthy split of whatever they took at the door, and I accepted their offer.

In the month prior to the opening there had been no little interest in the link with Uncle Richard and I did several interviews on the subject, which came as a surprise. The press were clearly interested in the connection with me, him and Dylan Thomas.

At this point in my career, I had been reluctant to use the connection with Uncle Rich to help me and had managed, pretty much, to keep it out of play. I was determined to make my reputation off my own back, but now I was faced with a different situation: I was doing a solo version of a work that was synonymous with the name Richard Burton – and *he* happened to be my uncle. The tie-in was far too much to play down and would turn out to be a serious ticket seller for this particular play. People and the press seemed to be genuinely interested if I was happy to talk about it, nearing ten years since Richard's death, the anniversary was a big selling point.

I'm sure we all have a few significant moments in life which can be labelled 'turning points'. The night of my Traverse Theatre opening in Edinburgh was one of them.

I was reviewed by the notorious weekly arts programme, *The Usual Suspects* on Radio Scotland, who had selected my show as their main focus for the week. I'd heard the trails in the days before: 'And on Wednesday night, our band of critics will be heading to the Traverse to see a one-man version of *Under Milk Wood* by Dylan Thomas. How is one man going to do it? Well, we're going to find out!' The tone was ominous and verging, very definitely, on the sarcastic. Clearly there was scepticism and I genuinely wondered if I was in for a roasting and, why-oh-why, had I dragged Richard's name into it? By linking myself to him, I was surely putting myself in the firing line...

Before the show I was sick with nerves, something I'd suffered before (but I have never done since) and trembling behind the curtain as the overture swelled. I wobbled on during the blackout...

I don't remember too much about the performance except that someone laughed in the opening monologue which nearly threw me. But then, when I got to 'neddying among the snuggeries of babies,' I heard a sigh. An audible sigh! A sigh of pure enchantment and it was at this point that I just let go. I let it all flow out of me; for the next ninety-five minutes, with no let up. No interval. Just Llareggub, pouring out, unexpurgated. And when the lights finally faded down, there was a looooong silence... and then... they all stood. Every one of them. They stood as one and cheered! They actually *cheered*! That had never happened to me before. I had no idea what had happened. Something just clicked.

The eventual live radio review was like nothing I'd ever heard. Elegiac. A stream of praise from everyone that went on and on and on. I had a hit on my hands.

The very next day, I was invited to perform at the Edinburgh Festival later that year by the prestigious Assembly Rooms where the entire run sold out prior to the opening performance. From there, I was invited all around the United Kingdom, to Israel, New Zealand, Australia, the Caribbean, Washington DC, on the QE2. You name it, and I probably did it. I've never counted, but I've never tired of it.

Looking back I'm still trying to figure out what makes the show a success, and I suppose I can only put it down to an amalgam or an alchemy, if you like, of Dylan Thomas's extraordinary words with my ability to perform them without interfering with them or trying to be too clever. Maybe the audience get more of my solo rendition than others which are cast with more than one actor but inevitably too few actors to cover all the parts? Perhaps problems occur when the audience become distracted from Dylan's words by thoughts of who is playing who – 'Oh, is that Mr Pugh? Isn't that the same actor that just played Mr Ogmore?' Or, 'Ah, Myfanwy Price... Oh, no it's not, it's Bessie Bighead!' Maybe they are more preoccupied figuring out what's going on than listening to the words and my uncomplicated version, with one actor playing all the parts is clearer? Maybe, once they get over the slightly disconcerting idea that the entire piece is being delivered by a baldy bloke in flannel pyjamas, they just start to listen... just as Dylan himself asks us to do in the opening monologue: 'Listen... Listen... Look.'

In touring the world giving my performance of this most enduring and magical work, I was asked, very often, to give recitals of other Dylan Thomas works such as his poetry and short stories. I would oblige as best I could and, carrying the omnibus edition of his collected works on my trips, I'd work on a request basis. After a few years and having given a few hundred of these recitals, I found that I had passively committed his most requested works to memory. In 2001, I decided to actively collate a new solo performance of all my favourites – three short stories and eleven poems – entitling the event, *Fern Hill & Other Dylan Thomas*. The show was to illustrate the wonderfulness of Dylan's 'other works' – the 'Not Under Milk Wood' works – and my remit on this occasion, just as with *Under Milk Wood*, was simply to learn the words and interpret them through my imagination. Certainly not to read them from a book as I had been doing.

I soon found that the stories, written in the first person, became incredibly personal and I was telling them as if they were my own stories, slices of my own history. Maybe this is how all good stories work? That they become our own when we read them. The images that theses stories conjured soon became akin to my own memories and, in performing them, I gave free rein to this. As an actor, there is no stronger force than to recall your own truth. Indeed, if you learn something well enough, the truth of the characters you are playing can become your own, and this is how I performed them.

The show was, very surprisingly, another big hit and won several prestigious awards. More to the point, it proved to me the enduring brilliance and wonderfulness of Dylan Thomas, and my belief in that his words should be heard rather than read. Indeed, as proven by Richard Burton and Thomas himself, his words fly at you with an intrinsic energy that entrances, mesmerises and enchants, and I'm sure that he wrote them in the full belief that that is exactly what they would do. He 'designed' them that way.

People often ask me why I am still performing *Under Milk Wood* after twenty-one years. Well, the simple answer is because I still love it. So much so, in fact, that I can't imagine my life without it. I believe that Dylan Thomas was a true genius the likes of which we will rarely see again, and it pains me to think of what we lost, what the world lost, when he died at the age of thirty-nine. What little I can do to ensure that his work is not forgotten I am happy, no, honoured, to do. By proxy, I get to earn my keep doing something I absolutely love to do because every time I get on that stage to say his words, I just can't wait. It is such an honour to be allowed to do it, and it is an incredible thought that I might just be the only person in the entire world who knows all those words, in the right order (well, most of the time) and sobering to think that I am most definitely the only one in the world nuts enough to try it! Ah, well, I guess someone had to. I'm just glad it was me.

Stealing a Slice, Staking Our Claim

Jon Gower

After Dylan we were all living under Milk Wood. If you lived in an average Welsh village after that beguiling and seductive play for voices had made itself very well known to the world, you were almost duty bound to look for the matching archetypes among the inhabitants. It was a game we simply had to play in my home village of Pwll, just as they did in Trimsaran, Llangennech and all the others.

Mrs Ogmore-Prichard. Oh, she's like that deputy headmistress who lives up on Top Road: she'd force the sun to wipe its shoes before coming inside, sure as eggs is eggs. Any sea dog, or even someone who'd simply once cruised the sea-shore one afternoon in a pedalo had to be become *our* Captain Cat. (Luckily we had an entire Sailors' Row in our village, from the days before they moved the sea, or rather Isambard Kingdom Brunel separated the village from the sea by building the London to Carmarthen railway along the estuary edge.)

Dylan underlined the value of local characters at a time when they had just started to be a disappearing race, as homogeneity started to hold sway. He gave us the archetypes and we tested the template against the populace around us. So Pwll had its own Polly Garter, Bessie Bighead and Rosie Probert, talked of, disapprovingly and in hushed tones, by chapel-goers garbed in Biblical black.

In Pwll, on the south Wales coast, two miles west of Llanelli, we had already assembled a pretty rich cast of Thomasesque or Thomasian characters in advance of the play's attempt at world domination. The tatterdemalion bunch of Pwllites (broadly like the Hittites, only Welsh speaking) included Texas Dan, a venerable and rangy tramp who wore a broad-rimmed Stetson hat both indoors and outside. Now, he'd only been to the Yew-knighted-States for some six months – and nobody every quite worked out why he went, although he would sometimes hint at fortunes made in oil – yet his accent was as broad as the Panhandle.

One day he found the body of a murdered nurse in Stradey Woods.

Local legend has it that when he panted his way into the local police station (in the days when such fabled places still pertained) he asked 'Are you the sheriff in these here parts? Because if you are you'd better rustle up a posse coz there's a stiff up in the canyon...' And then there was Clocsi, who hammered iron nails through the soles of his wooden clogs and then went fishing out in the estuary at low tide, spearing flat fish with his soles, if you pardon the pun. With such a rare parade of people on permanent display, sometimes we had grounds to maintain that Llareggub had bugger all on us. And there were others, so many others. But they, the local characters were dying out, as many people argued. Thus *Under Milk Wood* was both a document of village life and an elegy, too for the sort of people who were passing from us.

The reality of growing up in a village called Pwll, which translates as 'pit' or 'hole' was such that we probably craved with all heart the attention lavished on Dylan's fictional place. And like many a village we tried to claim our own bit of the Dylan legend, a little bit of his stardust.

I'm not sure when I fell under Dylan's thrall. I remember someone reading 'Fern Hill' and then enjoying all the poems, one-by-one, mystified by the ones like crossword puzzles but entranced beyond measure by a half dozen of them, maybe the half dozen poems that truly soar, that seem to go beyond sense and this known world, taking not just the reader with them, but *the very soul* of the reader.

Having read much of the work I progressed to reading tales about their shaper, devouring all the available biographies, before moving on to the stories. I adored the myriad ways in which he rhymed and chimed, found the euphonious in the everyday, took a tuning fork to vocabulary and helped make songs in a sublime register. And not just ordinary singing, but silver chimes of ousel song or whatever melodious bird was on hand. Dylan, the drunken sot besotted by language, cast a spell. If there was any doubt about his enduring influence on me then I need only quote the opening paragraph of my 2010 novel *Uncharted*:

> *Listen! Like a million small, slippery wet kisses on muddy*
> *shore and hard escarpment, on pebble beach and marshy*

reaches, the enormous river meets the land and sings to it, a
song of love, water to earth. It is a polyphonic symphony
with a chorus of aqueous voices – sucking seductions, rip-
pling percussions, and millions of swamp frogs looking for
a wet date. This is the river song. Cancion del Rio.

Listen, similarly, as Dylan parades the world of night-time
Llareggub:

Listen. It is night moving in the streets, the processional
salt slow musical wind in Coronation Street and Cockle Row,
it is the grass growing on Llareggub Hill, dewfall, starfall,
the sleep of birds in Milk Wood.

Listen. It is night in the chill, squat chapel, hymning in
bonnet and brooch and bombazine black, butterfly choker and
bootlace bow, coughing like nannygoats, sucking mintoes,
fortywinking hallelujah; night in the four-ale, quiet as a
domino; in Ocky Milkman's lofts like a mouse with gloves;
in Dai Bread's bakery flying like black flour. It is to-night
in Donkey Street, trotting silent. With seaweed on its
hooves, along the cockled cobbles, past curtained fernpot,
text and trinket, harmonium, holy dresser, watercolours
done by hand, china dog and rosy tin teacaddy. It is night neddying among the snuggeries of babies.

Now I'm not making any claims for the quality of my prose, but
that imperative at the beginning of my novel is a direct nod to Dylan's
play for voices. Here's how my description of nocturnal Buenos Aires
continues:

Listen carefully, hush your very heart and you can hear a
broken syntax of fractured conversation – partial sentences,
snipped phrases...

It seems that sometime, way back in those teen years, Dylan Thomas planted the seed of the idea and many years later my imagination allowed it to flower, as a nocturne, a night-time picture of Buenos Aires, cast in orchidaceous if not florid prose: Llarregub, imagined, perhaps as Macondo.

But there were other elements of Dylan that appealed to me hugely. I grew up on the edge of the Loughor estuary, where the light is estuarine, reflected off acres of sand and mud in a way which is quite unlike the marine light of, say, Porthcawl or Aberystwyth. Here I spent my teenage years spotting birds on the salt-marshes, the pebble spits and huge expanses of flat sands, such as at Cefn Sidan, where sanderling, those tiny clockwork birds, patrolled the spume at the tide's edge. I was independent of spirit, as I imagined Dylan to be, as a young man.

So Dylan seemed a kindred spirit, observing the hawk hanging still above St. John's Hill just as I noted kestrels hovering over the marram-grassed acres of Pembrey saltings. He also noted, quite brilliantly, and with some reverence, it seemed to me, the 'heron priested' shore. Just as some people find their inspiration and spiritual sustenance on mountains, or hills I found mine in the muddy runnels and stickleback infested creeks of an estuary. I envied him the vista from the Boat House.

So, at night, worn out after too many miles of walking, I would rest by going on a vicarious nature ramble with Dylan, a bit of bird-watching among the verse, in the company of a poet who probably didn't use binoculars, or know the Latin names. Yet he assembles quite a check list, a veritable avifauna, flying through the poems, or, in his own words, 'palavers of birds'.

In the stanzas 'cormorants scud' and we see 'curlews aloud in the congered waves/work at their ways to death'. There are flocks of 'reverend rooks' and 'pleasure birds', 'silk pigeons' and 'planet-ducted pelicans'. There's a hawk on fire and finches that bravely 'fly in the claw tracks of hawks'.

But Thomas wasn't just attentive to the range of species. He was also a documentarian of nature's cycles and appearances, and could seemingly mimic the hoot owl, with a 'grassblade blown in cupped hands' and note the delicate, fish-calmingly steady way the heron proceeds along the mud, 'ankling the scaly lowlands of the waves...'

And there is the forever sense of seasonality. Summer, of course, has its 'swallow thronged' lofts and 'nightjars flying with the ricks' and owls that can bear the farm away.

Autumn, slightly paradoxically, comes with 'a springful of larks in a rolling/Cloud and the roadside bushes brimming with whistling/Blackbirds and the sun of October/summery'... and Sir John's Hill dons a black cap of jackdaws. And then comes 'A Winter's Tale' with its 'puffed birds hopping and hunting' and its nightingale, that archetypical bird of summer, now turned 'dust in the buried wood'. In passing, it's moot to point out that the shade of Dylan Thomas would be hard pressed to hear a nightingale in the woods of Carmarthenshire nowadays: this perfect songster has pretty much fled the land, a bird now extinct in Wales.

So, here was a man who knew the natural world in a deep and intimate manner, who could use the fundamental human resource, language, to engage with it and explore its reality and metaphysics. He also liked his beer, as I was learning to do, supping elicit pints of nutmeg-tasting Felinfoel in the Farrier's Arms, hidden away in Stradey Woods. So we had that in common, a love of libation and bitter-induced conversation.

And then there was the Dylan Thomas voice, aqueous, liquid, like the voice a pint of Guinness would have were it able to ventriloquize. At times it had all the depth and mystery of ocean's undertow, while at others it had the ripe potential of exploding fruit. Little wonder that so many people have read his work in a pale and parodic imitation of Dylan's declaiming. His voice was a seduction in and of itself. And then, to add to his allure, there were the other seductions, hinted at by his biographers, not least when he went careening around America, where they lapped him up. Oh there were so many reasons to love Dylan! Everybody wanted a slice, a piece of the action, a souvenir that said 'Dylan was/slept/slurred here.' And we were not immune from this in our village...

When I grew up there was talk that he'd stayed in Pwll, in the big house on the hill overlooking the village. Later on, when I was old enough to hear such racy talk, the rumour deepened: Dylan had been having an affair with the daughter of Cilymaenllwyd House. No! Really? Duw, duw! Scarcely believe. At that time I just presumed that it was the village equivalent to an urban myth, like the vanishing hitchhiker, or a case of Lloyd George knew my father, or Gladstone stayed here: more wish fulfillment than steamy, sordid reality (not that I knew much about the latter in my tender, sheltered years in Pwll).

In Dylan's day the daughter of Cilymaenllwyd House, which stands on a green hump of land overlooking the Burry estuary, was Margaret Howard Stepney, born with a fanfare in 1913, when the townspeople of nearby Llanelli chipped in to buy her an immaculately crafted silver cradle. Known familiarly as Marged Fach, she was born with a silver spoon in her mouth to go with the ornately decorated cradle, and grew up to become a debutante who eventually had two marriages. She was also a member of the small army of patrons who kept Dylan on his feet, if a little unsteadily.

Dylan's wife Caitlin described her with barely contained bitterness, recalling nights when she would be alone with Dylan, reading aloud, when the phone would go. It would be Marged who '... came from a family that claimed descent from the Tudors. Marged had inherited huge estates in Carmarthenshire from her mother and lived in a large house near Llanelli. She was a cousin of Richard *A High Wind in Jamaica* Hughes's wife, Frances; she had been married twice, and was a year older than Dylan. We got to know her as "his best friend in the world", which I thought was pure wishful thinking; we only knew her for a short time.'

The determined Marged would attend the poet's readings in London and Caitlin believed that she was doing her level best to have an affair with him. She claimed that Marged had already had an affair with John Davenport and had doubt whatsoever that she would have happily bedded down with Dylan given half a chance. 'Although she was stinking rich, Marged was a really low alcoholic and used to go around with a kind of keeper woman.'

Marged did become Milk Woodishly eccentric, her odd behaviour shored up by the family cash. She dismayed her advisers by handing out presents to the needy not to mention spending time drinking with Dylan Thomas when she could. Seemingly there was some sort of chemistry between them, as the following letter, probably written in 1952, comes from a heavily altered worksheet, and was probably never sent.

My dear Marged, You told me once, upon a time, to call on you when I was beaten down, and you would try to pick me up. Maybe I should not have remembered...

Once upon a time you told me,
I remember in my bones,
That when the bad world had rolled me
Over on the scolding stones,
Shameless, lost, as the day I came
I should with my beggar's cup
Howl down the wind and call your name
And you, you raise me up.

The same very same time I told you,
And swore by heart & head,
That I would forever hold you
To the lovely words you said:
I never thought so soon I'd lie
Lonely in the whining dust;
My one wish to love and die,
But life is all mustn't and must...

I mustn't love, & I must die
But only when I am told,
But Fear sits in the mansioned sky,
And the winged Conventions scold,
And Money is the dunghill King

And his royal nark is the dun;
And dunned to death I write this jingling thing
Damned to death in the dear sun.
The jingling thing.

There's a clue in the poem, perhaps to the depth of Marged and Dylan's friendship. Typically cryptic, but with a lilt and line all of its own, this was not the sort of poem you'd craft to someone you'd just met. I well remember reading it out to a small audience of people in Pwll Community Centre and apart from the pleasure they derived from Dylan's euphony there was also a sense of validation. That the village was worth at least a footnote in the history of Wales's most famous poet was worth a lot, especially after history stole Amelia Earhart from us (the pioneering aviatrix landed off Pwll after crossing the Atlantic but because her plane was towed into nearby Burry Port, and she thus made landfall there, Pwll's role in her aerial adventures was completely overlooked).

But Dylan was also skint and Marged had cash. In a letter in February 1953 to Charles Fry, of the publishers Allan Wingate Dylan wrote: 'Early this year, my best friend in the world, a woman of my own age, died of drink and drugs. And I've been ill, too.' He referred to her as that 'Marged Gin Woman' who had died in London on 22 January. The resulting inquest was told she had suffocated after a dose of sleeping pills: the verdict was misadventure. Marged had intended to take over the Boat House from Margaret Taylor (the wife of the eminent historian A.J.P. Taylor, another patron of Dylan's freewheeling and excessive lifestyle) and pay all of its expenses for Thomas family, but her financial advisers were being stern and prohibitive, making difficulties.

Marged had been with Dylan the night before she died. In a letter, written in the Boat House to John Alexander Rolph Dylan wrote: 'I do hope we'll have another evening soon without so many people and so much confusion. The thin pale woman with us – Marged Howard Stepney – who drank sherry very quickly, died the very next evening of an overdose of a sleeping drug.'

The impecunious Dylan had extra reason to grieve over Marged's passing. In a letter written the next day to John Malcolm Brinnin he referred to a promise the Cilymaenllwyd heiress would no longer be able to keep. 'Then a woman – you never met her – who drank sherry very quickly, died the very next evening of an overdose of a sleeping drug and left no will, and her son, their heir could hardly be expected to fulfill that kind of unwritten agreement.'

In this centenary year we all claim some part of him: the roistering poet, the incredibly hard-working fashioner of undying verse, the toper, the bore, the velvet-voiced broadcaster, the short story writer, determined compiler of acrostic and cryptogrammic verse, the war years' political propagandist, the nostalgia-drunk celebrant of childhood Christmases (in Wales, and elsewhere), the US touring lecturer and the vaudevillian in the groves of academe, the playwright, the lover, the pantheist, the Swansea boy. All these and more.

He is a convenient grail for literary tourism and one of the most famous Welshman, up there with Tom Jones and Ryan Giggs, and is some sort of validation for the rest of us. He's one of the three main poetic Thomases, standing higher in the pantheon than Edward and R.S., maybe because of the presence of those Cuban heels of celebrity, rather than in terms of qualitative comparison.

But for me, most of all, here was a supreme wordsmith, conjuring, like some Celtic shaman, a whole euphonious-sounding world into being, with his incantations and descants, his lovely lilts and glorious, sustaining and enduring songs. Yes, those songs, which soar like skylarks, making high the sky.

Contributors

Michael Bogdanov

Michael Bogdanov has directed Shakespeare in many of the world's leading theatres and with major companies including the Royal Shakespeare Company. He was Associate Director of the Royal National Theatre for eight years, before co-founding the English Shakespeare Company in 1986 with actor Michael Pennington. He was also Chief Executive of the Deutsches Schauspielhaus (National Theatre) in Hamburg, 1989-1992. He has won numerous awards including the Society of West End Theatres Best Director for his production of *The Taming of the Shrew* (RSC) and the Laurence Olivier Award for Best Director for his seven-play history cycle *The Wars of the Roses* (ESC). His work for film and television includes the documentary *Shakespeare on the Estate* and a ninety-minute feature film *A Light in the Valley*. Born of Russian and Welsh parentage, he lives in Cardiff and Hamburg.

D.J. Britton

D.J. Britton is Director of Studies in Creative Writing at Swansea University. An award-winning dramatist, director and dramaturg, he ran the Australian Broadcasting Corporation's radio drama department before moving to Wales. Since his first Australian stage play, *Landlovers*, he has written many works for theatre, radio and the visual media. Australian stage credits include *Cargo* (Swan Gold Play of the Year) and *Plainsong* (Equity Production of the Year). In Wales he has written and directed extensively for the BBC, National Theatre Wales and Sherman Cymru. He is Artistic Director of Theatr Cadair, formed to develop new theatre works in Wales following the success of his Lloyd George play *The Wizard, the Goat and the Man Who Won the War*. The Dylan Thomas centenary celebrations include a revival of his experimental sound-work, *Chelsea Dreaming*.

Horatio Clare

Horatio Clare's latest book is the widely acclaimed, ocean-spanning *Down to the Sea in Ships*. A writer, radio producer and journalist, Clare was born in London, though he and his brother Alexander grew up on a hill farm in the Black Mountains of south Wales. He worked at the BBC as a producer on *Front Row*, *Night Waves* and *The Verb* and has written two memoirs, *Running for the Hills* and *Truant: Notes from the Slippery Slope*. He has also penned a travel book, *A Single Swallow* as well as a retelling of one of the tales from the Mabinogion as *The Prince's Pen*. He wrote and edited *Sicily Through Writers' Eyes* and is a contributor to the collections *Red City: Marrakech Through Writers' Eyes* and *Meetings With Remarkable Muslims*.

Dai George

Dai George was born in Cardiff in 1986 and has studied in Bristol and New York, where he received a Masters in Fine Art from Columbia University's famous writing programme. Now living and teaching in London, but often back in Wales, he has had poems and critical articles published in *The Guardian online*, *The Boston Review*, *Poetry Wales*, *New Welsh Review* and others. His poetry has appeared in several anthologies, including the *Salt Book of Younger Poets* and *Best British Poetry* (2011 and forthcoming in 2013). He is at work on a novel about the Gunpowder Plot, starring the playwright Ben Jonson as a central character.

Sarah Gridley

Sarah Gridley is an Assistant Professor at Case Western Reserve University in Cleveland, Ohio where she has been poet in residence as well as teaching poetry at all levels. Educated initially at the universities of Harvard and Tufts she then gained her MFA in writing poetry from the University of Montana. Her books include *Loom*, *Green is the Orator* and *Weather Eye Open*. Sarah Gridley's poems have appeared in various journals, including *Crazyhorse*, *Denver Quarterly*, *Gulf Coast*, *jubilat*, *Kenyon Review Online*, *New American Poetry*, and *Slope*. She is also a recent recipient of an Individual Excellence Award from the Ohio Arts Council, and a Creative Workforce Fellowship from the Community Partnership for Arts and Culture.

Jon Gower

Jon Gower is a writer and broadcaster who has seventeen books to his name: these include the novel *Y Storïwr*, which won the Wales Book of the Year in 2012, the coastal journey *Wales: At Water's Edge*, which was shortlisted for the 2013 prize and *The Story of Wales*, which accompanies the landmark BBC television series. He has also written travel books such as *An Island Called Smith*, an account of a disappearing island in Chesapeake Bay, as well as five collections of short stories in both Welsh and English. He is a former BBC Wales arts and media correspondent, was an inaugural Hay Festival International Fellow, has won a major Creative Wales award and is a Fellow of the Welsh Academy.

Steve Groves

Cardiff born and bred, journalist Steve Groves has held most posts on regional newspapers in south Wales – as a leader writer, political editor, industrial editor and was for many years a regular and popular columnist for the *Western Mail*. During a long career in broadcasting he has produced an array of programmes for BBC Radio 4, BBC Radio 2, the BBC World Service and BBC Radio Wales on a wide range of subjects from the arts through history and current affairs to sport and politics. He has also been Chief News Assistant at Radio Wales and acting editor of Radio Wales News. Steve is now a freelance radio producer, sound recordist, arts' collaborator and occasional lecturer and is currently working on a current affairs series for Radio Wales about newspapers and the 'democratic deficit'.

Sarah King

Sarah King is a writer, journalist and art critic. She has a background in history and travel writing and currently writes for *Wales Arts Review*. Her first screenplay is in pre-production and she is also working on her first stage play. After living in Australia, Denmark, Zambia, Tanzania and England she settled in Wales ten years ago, and now lives in Cardiff.

Andrew Lycett

Andrew Lycett is an English biographer and journalist. He was educated at Charterhouse School and studied modern history at Christ Church, Oxford and edited Cherwell, the university newspaper. He then worked for a while for The Times as a correspondent in Africa, the Middle East, and Asia. He has written several well-received biographies of the Libyan leader Colonel Muammar Qadaffi, the stockbrokers George Rowe & Frederick I. Pitman, Rudyard Kipling, Wilkie Collins, Sir Arthur Conan Doyle and Dylan Thomas: A New Life. He is perhaps best known for his biography of Ian Fleming, *Ian Fleming: The Man Behind James Bond*. He was elected a Fellow of the Royal Society of Literature in 2009 and is also a Fellow of the Royal Geographical Society.

Guy Masterson

Guy Masterson is an Olivier Award winning producer, actor, director and writer. An entertainer for thirty years, he has worked on over 150 shows. He is one of the most highly-awarded independent presenters at the Edinburgh Fringe Festival. As a theatre director, he is responsible for several of its biggest hits. As an actor he is globally renowned for his solo performances, including *Fern Hill & Other Dylan Thomas*. In 2003, he worked with composer Matt Clifford to add music and soundscape to his production of *Under Milk Wood* for the Edinburgh Festival and then embarked on a major tour to mark the 50th anniversary of Dylan Thomas's death. He has recently adapted *Animal Farm* which he will direct in Tbilisi, Georgia in 2014, a year that will also see the premiere of a new solo work, *Anthem for Doomed Youth* in Edinburgh.

Kaite O'Reilly

Kaite O'Reilly has won many prizes for her work, including the Ted Hughes Award for new works in poetry for her version of Aeschylus's *Persians* for National Theatre Wales. In 2012 she received two Cultural Olympiad Commissions for *In Water I'm Weightless*, produced by National Theatre Wales/South Bank Centre as part of the official festival celebrating the London Olympics/Paralympics. In 2014 she will have productions in translation in Estonia, Belgium, Taiwan, and Hong Kong, and a UK tour of *Woman of Flowers*, her retelling of The Mabinogion's Blodeuwedd for Forest Forge. She has written extensively for radio and is now completing her first novel, *A Sky Without Stars*, a poignant, funny novel seen through the eyes of the younger daughter of Irish immigrants to Birmingham during the IRA activity of 1973/4. She will begin work on her second novel in 2015, thanks to a Literature Wales bursary.

Gary Raymond

Gary Raymond is the Senior Editor of *Wales Arts Review*, and has had published a diverse range of fiction, arts and literary criticism, travelogue and journalism. As well as a regular voice in *Wales Arts Review*, and being Wales's theatre critic for London's *The Arts Desk*, Gary has written for publications such as *The Guardian*, *Rolling Stone Magazine* and the *Western Mail*, and is a regular contributor to local and national BBC radio on the subject of arts and culture. In 2013, Gary published *J.R.R. Tolkien: A Visual Biography of Fantasy's Most Revered Writer* with Ivy Press. Gary is also a lecturer in English and Creative Writing at the University of South Wales.

Jeff Towns

Jeff Towns, a.k.a. 'The Dylan Thomas Guy', is a rare-book dealer based in Swansea who, for more than forty years, from his Dylans Bookstores in and around the city, has specialized in books about Wales in all its many aspects. He is currently the Chairman of the Dylan Thomas Society of Great Britain. Not content with selling books he also now produces them: these include editing and introducing *A Pearl of Great Price: The Love Letters of Dylan Thomas to Pearl Kazin* and, with Wyn Thomas compiling *Dylan Thomas – The Pubs*, a guide to those hostelries where the poet could find 'a place of refuge; as a place of conviviality, warmth and shelter; as a theatre in which he could always be counted on to perform, and always be guaranteed an audience!'

George Tremlett

George Tremlett is an English author, rock journalist, a former politician – serving on the Greater London Council – and bookshop owner, who has run the Corran bookshop in Laugharne, described as a 'shrine to the poet' since the early 1980s. After leaving King Edward VI School in Stratford-upon-Avon he worked for the *Coventry Evening Telegraph* before becoming a freelance contributor to *New Musical Express* and other music publications. He was David Bowie's first biographer and has written no fewer than seventeen music biographies, including: John Lennon, Marc Bolan, David Essex, Slade Rod Stewart, Cliff Richard, Queen, Paul McCartney, The Rolling Stones and The Who. He has also penned books about the lives of both Dylan and Caitlin, and also, with James Nashold, speculated about what caused *The Death of Dylan Thomas*.

Rachel Trezise

Rhondda-based Rachel Trezise's first novel, *In and Out of the Goldfish Bowl*, was published in 2000 and selected for the Orange Futures list. *Fresh Apples* (2005) followed, a collection short stories celebrating youth, which won the inaugural EDS Dylan Thomas Prize. Her third book, *Dial M for Merthyr* (2007) is a travelogue and appreciation of Midasuno, a Merthyr rock band. Rachel also wrote the script for *I Sing of a Maiden*, performed in Chapter Arts Centre in 2007, a conversation exploring teenage pregnancy. In 2008, her first radio play, *Lemon Meringue Pie*, was broadcast on BBC Radio 4 while in 2013, National Theatre Wales staged her first full length work for the stage, *Tonypandemonium*. Her most recent books are a second novel, *Sixteen Shades of Crazy* and a collection of short stories, *Cosmic Latte*.

Other titles available from The H'mm Foundation

R.S. Thomas – poet, priest, nationalist – came to dominate the Welsh literary scene in the second half of the twentieth and was nominated for the Nobel Prize for Literature.

Published on the centenary of his birth, these essays show the many ways in which both the man and the poetry inspired affection and admiration in others.

With contributions from:
Gillian Clarke
Fflur Dafydd
Grahame Davies
Gwyneth Lewis
Peter Finch
Jon Gower
Menna Elfyn
Osi Rhys Osmond
Jeff Towns
M. Wynn Thomas
Alex Salmond
Archbishop of Wales Barry Morgan

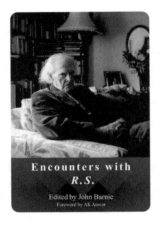

Encounters with R.S. | £9.99
978-0-9927560-0-0
Edited by John Barnie

Other titles available from The H'mm Foundation

Nigel Jenkins – poet, encyclopaedist, campaigner, performer, gifted teacher and superb prose stylist – was a man of Gower, of Swansea and – in the deepest sense possible – of Wales.

Published in the year of his untimely and all too premature passing, *Encounters with Nigel* gathers tributes, critical essays and poems by fellow poets, prose practitioners and former students. Together they explore many sides of a fascinating man, who had an uncommon generosity of spirit not to mention the best reading voice this side of the Urals.

With contributions from:
Fflur Dafydd
John Barnie
M. Wynn Thomas
Mike Parker
Stevie Davies
Daniel G. Williams
Iwan Bala
D.J. Britton
Robert Minhinnick
Jane Fraser
Humberto Gatica

Encounters with
Nigel

Edited by Jon Gower
Foreword by Ali Anwar

Encounters with Nigel | £9.99
978-0-9927560-4-8
Edited by Jon Gower

You can buy this title from www.thehmmfoundation.co.uk
also available as an ebook on amazon.co.uk